ESTIMATING
FOREIGN RESOURCE NEEDS
FOR ECONOMIC DEVELOPMENT

THEORY, METHOD, AND
A CASE STUDY OF COLOMBIA

ECONOMICS HANDBOOK SERIES

SEYMOUR E. HARRIS, EDITOR

Burns   Social Security and Public Policy

Carlson   Economic Security in the United States

Duesenberry   Business Cycles and Economic Growth

Fisher   The Identification Problem in Econometrics

Hansen   A Guide to Keynes

Hansen   The American Economy

Hansen   The Dollar and the International Monetary System

Hansen   Economic Issues of the 1960s

Hansen   Monetary Theory and Fiscal Policy

Harris   International and Interregional Economics

Harrod   The British Economy

Henderson and Quandt   Microeconomic Theory

Hoover   The Location of Economic Activity

Johnston   Statistical Cost Analysis

Kindleberger   Economic Development

Lebergott   Manpower in Economic Growth

Lerner   Economics of Employment

Phelps   Fiscal Neutrality Toward Economic Growth

Taylor   A History of Economic Thought

Theil, Boot, and Kloek   Operations Research and Quantitative Economics

Tinbergen and Bos   Mathematical Models of Economic Growth

Vanek   Estimating Foreign Resource Needs for Economic Development

Walton and McKersie   A Behavioral Theory of Labor Negotiations

ESTIMATING
FOREIGN RESOURCE NEEDS
FOR ECONOMIC DEVELOPMENT

THEORY, METHOD, AND
A CASE STUDY OF COLOMBIA

JAROSLAV VANEK
PROFESSOR OF ECONOMICS
CORNELL UNIVERSITY

WITH THE ASSISTANCE OF
RICHARD BILSBORROW

McGRAW-HILL BOOK COMPANY

NEW YORK   ST. LOUIS   SAN FRANCISCO   TORONTO   LONDON   SYDNEY

**ESTIMATING FOREIGN RESOURCE NEEDS
FOR ECONOMIC DEVELOPMENT**

To My Wife

PREFACE

Most of this study was written under the auspices of the United States Agency for International Development. I am grateful to the Agency both for its support and for its permission to publish the material. While with the Agency, I greatly benefitted from my association with Professor Hollis Chenery, whose influence on the study was truly decisive. Professor Seymour Harris suggested a number of important improvements for which I am very thankful. I am also grateful to Richard Bilsborrow for his indefatigable work as economist, statistician, and translator. Of course, the responsibility for all the views that I have expressed and for any possible mistakes is entirely mine.

This study is neither an exercise in theoretical elegance nor an example of econometric erudition. Rather, it represents a piece of unavoidably crude work whose sole justification for publication, if any, is the extreme seriousness of the problem treated.

JAROSLAV VANEK

CONTENTS

ESTIMATING
FOREIGN RESOURCE NEEDS
FOR ECONOMIC DEVELOPMENT

THEORY, METHOD, AND
A CASE STUDY OF COLOMBIA

PART **1**   THE GROUNDWORK

Chapter **1** INTRODUCTION

1-1 THE PURPOSE AND SCOPE OF THE STUDY

At least two-thirds of the world's population are living today under conditions of extreme poverty. Economic development of countries where such conditions prevail, without any doubt, is the most important and most pressing socioeconomic problem of our generation. Although this is the reality, our understanding of the development process, and thus our ability to design programs that would rapidly remedy the situation, is rather inadequate.

One of the few notions that development policy makers and development scientists are quite certain about is that economic development requires a substantial increase in national investment, that is, an accelerated rate of capital formation. Another such notion is that rapid economic development generally calls for a substantial volume of imports of materials, capital goods, and technical services. If, then, either exports are insufficient to finance such imports or domestic savings are insufficient to finance an increased volume of investment, or both (as is often the case), rapid development cannot be attained. In such situations, which are encountered in the early stages of development by virtually every economy, the only way out of the impasse is the substitution of foreign resources, in the form of public or private funds, for deficient savings and/or exports. The present study is addressed to the problems raised by this fundamental necessity.

Specifically, the author's purpose is to explore, both in theory and in practice, the interdependence between economic development and the requirements of foreign resources called for by that development. The subject matter can be classified under three distinct headings. First, a basic method of estimating foreign resource requirements for development, along with several subsidiary methods, is designed, tailored, so to speak, to the rather limited and inaccurate statistical information currently available for the majority of less developed countries. Second, the author applies the method in studying a concrete case, that of the Colombian economy, and thus, besides producing a set of useful estimates for that country, the author provides the reader with a detailed illustration. Third, an attempt is made to accommodate or extend existing economic theory to the specific problem of foreign resource requirements of developing countries.

The organization of the work reflects the inherent character of a case study. First, upon examination of available data, not only for Colombia but for a large number of developing countries, a simple but operational method of forecasting is designed. This is further explained in section 1-2. Next, this method is applied to the specific case of Colombia, resulting in a set of structural equations, which are then used in computing various estimates of future foreign resource requirements in Part 2. In the process of deriving the estimating model several methodological and theoretical problems arose, calling for separate—and in some cases quite extensive—treatment. Moreover, some interesting avenues of development analysis came to light as a by-product of the projection structure for Colombia. These, together with the more important theoretical and methodological aspects of the study, are further outlined in section 1-3, whereas most of the theoretical analysis is carried out in Part 3.

1-2 THE BASIC ESTIMATION PROCEDURE

In this section the basic method of estimating the foreign resource requirements for economic development is explained. Most conveniently, this exposition can be made in four stages. First, the heart of the matter is shown by a simple graphical schema. Although this "nutshell" presentation is a good deal simpler than the approach which we use in this study, it is very useful for three reasons: (1) It shows the very essentials whereon all methods of estimating foreign resource requirements, including our own, are based; (2) it permits us to identify easily the generalizations and refinements introduced in the method used; (3) it describes quite faithfully an approach which has often been employed by other students of economic development in tackling the problem at hand.

Next, using the schematic presentation as a point of departure, the author approaches the method used in this study in general terms and discusses its rationale.   In the third stage the author very briefly goes over some more advanced structures which in theory would be applicable in dealing with the proposed problem, but which, upon preliminary examination, were found in practice inapplicable—for the time being at least—to most, if not all, developing economies.   The remainder of this section is devoted to a more detailed presentation of the statistical relationships underlying our estimation procedure.

The basic schema permitting us to identify and ultimately to compute the foreign resource requirements of a developing country is nothing but the expression of a rudimentary theory of economic development.   As indicated by the three blocks on the right side of Figure 1 and the arrows

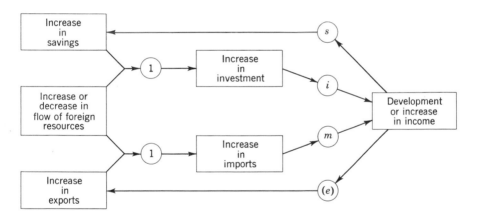

Figure 1.   Schematic representation of the procedure for estimating the foreign resource requirements of economic development.

connecting them, economic development calls for two key inputs: investment and imports.   To expand the national product by, say, 50 per cent over a given period, a less developed country must expand annual investment by, say, 100 per cent over that period and imports by 70 per cent. These relationships (namely, 100:50 and 70:50, respectively) represented in the schema by the terms i and m, respectively, can be taken, for the moment at least, as given parameters or constants.   We shall return a little later to these parameters in greater detail.

Now neither investment nor imports for a given period are unlimited. The former must equal the sum of savings S and foreign resources (aid and foreign capital funds) F; the latter must equal the availability of foreign exchange composed of export earnings E and foreign resources F. Thus S and F can be conceived of as necessary inputs into I; and E and F, necessary inputs into M.   The arrows and coefficients "1" in the schema indicate these relationships.

Finally, it will be observed that the system is in part a closed one in that two out of the three initial inputs, S, F, and E, are related to the output, that is, to the level of development and national product V.   As indicated in the diagram, savings depend on the level of national product V, the key coefficient relating changes in the two magnitudes being s.   As with i and m, the parameter s can, for the moment, be conceived of as a given constant.   The change in exports of the developing country is also linked, through an index of proportionality e, to development of that country. The interpretation of the index e, however, is somewhat different from that of i, m, and s, and for that reason it is bracketed.   Actually, the value of exports depends only in part on the conditions in the developing country; another and often a more important determinant of E is the conditions of demand abroad.

It is now clearly apparent from the schema that with given (statistically measured) initial levels of the magnitudes V, I, M, S, and E and a prescribed expansion of V such as the 50 per cent in our example above, the foreign resource requirements F can be calculated for a future period once we know (1) i and s, or (2) m and e, or (3) both (1) and (2).   As an example, in case (1) suppose that with $s = 0.15$ and $i = 0.20$, the initial levels are $V_0 = 1,000$, $I_0 = 200$, and $S_0 = 150$ (implying $F_0 = 50$), and a 50 per cent expansion in V is postulated between the base period and a projection period 10 years hence.   In this situation, $V_{10} = 1,500$, $I_{10} = 200 + 0.2 \times 500 = 300$, and $S_{10} = 150 + 0.15 \times 500 = 225$, so that $F_{10} = 75$.

The alternatives (1), (2), and (3) characterize the three basic approaches used in estimating the foreign resource requirements of developing countries.   Approaches (1) and (2) are self-evident from the schema; with regard to approach (3), involving the estimation of F through both (1) and (2), let it further be noted that generally two different estimates of F will be obtained for a future period using the two methods.   This apparent inconsistency, however, can be resolved and explained, and, moreover, it can yield valuable information about the development process itself.   In this study we adopt basic approach

(3), and we devote a good deal of attention to the duality of gap estimates which this approach entails (see especially Chapter 6).

Given the basic schema, the problem of estimating the foreign resource requirements of economic development can be characterized by and reduced to one thing: estimating the values of the parameters s, i, e, and m (some or all, depending on the basic method adopted) for the period for which an evaluation of the foreign resource requirements is sought.

Although all the methods used in estimating the key parameters s, i, e, and m are based on empirical investigation of relationships that have prevailed in the past, they vary considerably in complexity and sophistication. The most important factor of this variation among the different procedures is what we may term their "structure content." To be more explicit, what differentiates the entire spectrum of methods of estimating the key parameters is how much, or what degree, of the structure of the economy for which foreign resource requirements are to be estimated is built into the estimation procedure.

Using this criterion, the simplest, and perhaps the most frequently used, procedure is one not including any structure whatsoever. In this procedure a single variable is used for each of the four key magnitudes in our schema—savings, investment, exports, and imports—and is related (except possibly for exports which may be considered given by foreign conditions) to a single independent (predetermined) variable, namely, the rate of economic development as measured by the expansion of national income. In this case only four parameters must be estimated to obtain s, i, e, and m. Most frequently then, the past performance of the developing economy is studied to obtain the marginal savings rate, the marginal capital-output coefficient, the rate of expansion of exports, and the marginal import rate, and it is postulated that these parameters would prevail over the period of prediction.

Improvement on this simple procedure has been obtained in some cases[1] through disaggregation, or building in of structure, of some of the dependent variables S, I, E, or M, a single independent variable—the rate of expansion of the national product—being retained. Thus, for example, imports of raw materials can be taken out of total imports, and two separate relationships, one for raw materials, the other for all remaining imports, can be estimated, both using the rate of growth of national product as the independent variable.

A serious drawback of the above procedure is that it is based on only a single piece of information about the nature of the development process —the rate of economic expansion of the whole economy—while omitting

[1] For example, see the estimates of foreign resource requirements of developing countries presented in the United Nations *World Economic Survey* for 1962.

entirely the structural transformation of the economy.   And yet, structural change is as important a feature of economic development as the aggregate rate of growth.   Suppose, for example, that corresponding to a given future expansion of gross national product two alternative development structures are envisaged, one being heavily industry-oriented, the other stressing development of the agricultural sector.   It is evident that the two alternatives will call for quite different levels of imports, the industry-oriented alternative carrying, for some time at least, a heavier import bill.   It is equally evident that if a single variable, the gross national product, is used to explain total imports and a single parameter is estimated from historical data to express this relationship, the parameter cannot provide a correct prediction of what will happen in the future for all possible development structures.

It is this imperfection, stemming from the absence of structural change from the estimation procedure, that the method employed in this study is designed to avoid.   In essence, starting from the basic notion that different sectors of the economy will have widely different impacts on—or relations with—national savings, investment, imports, and exports, we do not use a single independent variable, the national product, but rather several independent variables, the value-added (net product) aggregates, for various sectors of the economy.   Of course, these sectoral aggregates all add up to national product at factor cost.   Ideally the number of sectors used ought to be determined by considering the nature of the relationships between different sectors on the one hand and the key dependent variables S, I, E, and M on the other.   In practice, however, the most important consideration that determined our choice of the sectoral breakdown was the availability of statistical information necessary for the estimation of the parameters s, i, e, and m.

Thus, instead of a simple estimation function, which would correspond to our basic schema, of the form

$$Y = f(V) \tag{1-1}$$

where Y stands for savings, investment, exports, or imports and V stands for national product, we use a relation of the general form

$$Y = f(V_1, V_2, \ldots, V_n) \tag{1-2}$$

where V_j is the value-added by the jth sector in an economy composed of n productive sectors and f is read as "function of."   As we have already pointed out, the sum over all the V_j's equals the national product (income) at factor cost.   The V_j's are the basic independent variables of our procedure.   However, it must be noted, even at this point, that the logic of determination of savings, investment, exports, and imports suggests that in some cases other independent or predetermined variables must be included in the function f. Since this will be discussed in greater detail later in the study, let us only mention here as an example that if Y in relation (1-2) represents exports of the developing country, the function f must also include the terms of trade or the average export prices as an independent variable.

Once the relations of the type indicated by (1-2) are established, the foreign resource requirements F can be estimated, as explained above in the basic schema, from projected values of the V_j's. This means that instead of a single value of total national product called for by relation (1-1), n sectoral values-added must be given, or predetermined. This would at first seem to be a considerable complication. In reality, however, it proves to be an advantage. In most cases it is easier to make realistic forecasts regarding the rates of sectoral expansion than it is, in the absence of such projections, to predict the rate of economic development for the whole economy. Moreover, the development plans of most less advanced countries, almost without exception, contain sectoral targets for the planning period, and the target for the economy as a whole is only a derived figure.

But perhaps the most important factor rendering the sectoral, or structural, approach desirable is a wide scope of application in evaluating the foreign resource requirements of various alternatives for development. This type of analysis has been extensively used and explored in this study. In fact, very often the question is not to produce a single figure on what foreign resources a given developing country will need over a prescribed future period but rather to furnish several estimates, each corresponding to a different rate of development and/or to a different development structure. It is clear from the foregoing discussion that any prescribed rate of aggregate economic growth and development structure will call for some minimum amount of foreign resources in that if such resources were not forthcoming, that prescribed rate of expansion and structure would not be attainable. Such alternative minimum requirements can then be obtained through our estimation procedure based on the estimation functions indicated by relation (1-2).

The basic estimation procedure outlined thus far, and used in this study, is really only a first step toward a full structural approach. For example, it will be noted that the sectoral value-added aggregates V_j's, used here as the key independent variables, do not furnish any information about the structure of final demand—that is, expenditures—in the developing economy; thus it is impossible to directly ascertain the implications of a given final demand bill for the foreign resource requirements. To establish such a link, an input-output model would be necessary.[2]   Moreover, there is no direct consideration given in our method to relative sectoral values or to the efficiency of resource allocation.[3]   This, however, is less of a shortcoming for our specific purpose. Indeed our task is not to estimate foreign resource requirements of efficient paths of development nor to study the dynamic efficiency of economic growth; rather it is the far less ambitious task of finding the relation between a prescribed development pattern and the transfer of foreign resources warranting that development.

Although aware of these and other possible refinements of the estimation procedure, we have adopted the comparatively simpler structural method based on sectoral values-added V_j's and characterized by relation (1-2).   As we have already noted, this choice—given the whole spectrum of theoretical possibilities—was based primarily on the availability of statistical information.   A careful scrutiny of statistical sources for the majority of developing countries led us to the conclusion that the simplest approach, devoid of any structure [see the basic schema and relation (1-1)], would ordinarily leave a good deal of statistical information untapped.   On the other hand, we found that any more refined and more sophisticated approach could generally not be used for lack of statistical material, such as input-output information and other data.   But even for the very few developing countries where attempts have been made to estimate the interindustry flow parameters, such information is most often of so low a quality that any real improvement of results over those obtainable through our simple structural approach can hardly be hoped for.

We can now return to our estimation procedure, defined by the basic schema and relation (1-2), and discuss in greater detail the four key estimation functions, that is, the investment function, the savings function, the import function, and the export function.   All these functions, it will be recalled, are implicitly set forth in relation (1-2).

Each of the four key aggregates I, S, M, and E, characterized in their ideal form in relation (1-2) by Y, can be visualized as sums of subaggre-

---

[2] An input-output model is one showing how much of the production of a given economic sector is used in various other sectors as inputs and how much is left over for final consumption.   It ought to be noted that if input-output information is available, an input-output structure can easily be grafted onto our simpler method, and final demands can then be computed for any selected composition of the V_j's.   The key to this extension is the postulate that value-added in the jth sector V_j remains a constant proportion of the gross product of that sector.

[3] Although efficiency of resource allocation is not directly considered in our prediction model, some methodological and empirical results bearing on efficiency have been obtained as a by-product.   These are outlined in the following section and presented later in Part 2 of the study.

gates, each imputable to a particular sector of the economy; that is,

$$Y = Y_1 + Y_2 + \cdots + Y_n \tag{1-3}$$

where, for example, Y_2 stands for investment, savings, imports, or exports associated with the operation of the second sector. Still considering the ideal situation, the principal explanatory variable for each Y_j should be the value-added in the jth sector, that is, V_j. We can thus write

$$Y_j = f_j(V_j) \tag{1-4}$$

It must be stressed that what has just been shown is only the ideal set of functions, providing us with a backbone of the estimation procedure and with a point of departure in the practical task of establishing the equations. The actual estimation equations—such as those obtained in our study for Colombia—are bound to be different, to a greater or lesser degree, from the ideal for two major reasons. First, once the sectoral breakdown into n value-added subaggregates is selected, for no developing country would there be all the statistical data necessary to estimate what is strictly implied by relations (1-3) and (1-4). Second, in some cases, to be identified and further explained later in the study, what is implied in relations (1-3) and (1-4) may not even be the best formulation from the point of view of the logic of economic relationships. With these general remarks and the rationale of relations (1-3) and (1-4) in mind, we can now consider the specific forms of the four key estimation equations.

The investment function

The first question that arises is whether to consider the gross or net investment—and, by implication, whether to consider the gross or net savings—of the developing economy. As the case almost always is in the context of the present study, expediency takes precedence over theoretical considerations in our making this decision. Net investment data for developing countries are extremely hard to come by, and in the few instances where some estimates have been produced, they certainly do not inspire confidence. Therefore, investment I, which has thus far been treated without any further qualification, must be taken as gross investment for the purpose of the estimation procedure.

Relations (1-3) and (1-4) now assume the specific forms

$$I = I_1 + \cdots + I_n \tag{1-5}$$

and

$$I_j = f_j(V_j) \tag{1-6}$$

respectively.   The function f_j in our study is of two different kinds. The first, more conventional, is based on the postulate that to increase output of a particular sector by a certain amount per annum, there must be a proportional amount invested in that sector, the index of proportionality k_j being a constant to be estimated from historical data.[4] The other form of function f_j is even simpler: it is based on the postulate that investment in a given sector is proportional to the value-added in that sector, that is, to V_j, the index of proportionality also being a constant to be estimated from available statistical information.   This simple function proves preferable especially in cases such as the agricultural sector, where capital is not the factor of primordial importance.   In such situations, as the scrutiny of real data bears out, no clear relation between capital stock and output can generally be established, and proportionality between annual investment and value-added appears as a better hypothesis.   Probably the most significant reason why this is so is that— especially in developing countries—investment in the particular sectors (such as agriculture or housing) must be understood primarily as savings in kind rather than as generation of necessary productive capacity.

In many developing countries where detailed statistics regarding investment are available, the breakdown offered is one into investments by type of asset—such as dwellings, other construction, machinery, transportation equipment, and inventories—rather than by sector of economic activity.   In such a situation it is necessary to adjust the investment function in accordance with that breakdown: total gross investment has to be explained as a sum of investments into different categories of assets, and each of the categories has to be made dependent on some appropriate combination of sectoral values-added.   For example, investment in machinery can be explained by the value-added in manufacturing and mining; investment in inventories and dwellings, by total national product (or value-added); investment in transportation equipment, by the value-added in the transportation sector, and so forth.

Although this alternative approach, forced by the availability of statistical information, is inferior to the strictly sectoral approach, it has one compensating advantage.   This advantage, to which we shall turn in greater detail when we discuss the import function, resides in the fact that certain parts of the investment function can be used directly in the

[4] The coefficient k_j is really nothing but a special form of a marginal capital-output coefficient; however it must be noted that it is a coefficient based on gross rather than net investment.   This may introduce a bias in the estimates of future investment, especially in cases where the rate of growth for the observed past period whereon the estimate of k_j is based and the rate of growth for the projection period are widely different.   A good deal of attention is paid to this source of bias later in our study, and corresponding theory as well as correction factors are worked out to cope with that bias in Chapter 7.

import function. Suppose, for example, that for the target period an investment of $100 million into machinery is predicted. Then the imports of machinery, in a typical less developed country which is not an exporter of machinery, will be equal to 100 minus whatever the domestic output of machinery is in the target period. But, it will be noted, the domestic output of machinery is directly related to the value-added of the machinery-producing sector, which in turn is one of the predetermined (exogenous) variables (one of the V_j's) of the predictive structure.

The savings function

Although it is possible to visualize in theory a savings function which—according to our basic relations (1-3) and (1-4)—would be composed of components imputable to different individual sectors of economic activity (i.e., to the individual V_j's), the mechanism of savings formation in developing countries does not suggest such an approach, nor do data exist, as a general rule, which would permit that approach. Thus the savings function which we use in our estimation procedure becomes an important departure from the basic estimation equations (1-3) and (1-4).

The first distinction which must be made, and incorporated into the savings function, is that between gross and net savings, or, what is the same thing, between net savings and the consumption of reproducible productive resources—capital. We can write

$$S_g = S_n + S_d \qquad\qquad (1\text{-}7)$$

where the subscripts stand for gross, net, and depreciation of capital.

Although generally of very poor quality, historical data for S_d most often do exist for the developing countries. These data, then, must be used in designing an estimation function for S_d. Because depreciation is naturally related to past gross capital formation, the most logical avenue of approach is to seek some relationship between the depreciation figures and gross investment in one or more periods preceding the write-off year. Very often a statistically satisfactory relationship can be found between depreciation in time t and a moving average of gross investments over a past period stretching from t minus p to t minus q, where, as an example, p can be 10 years and q five years. If such a relationship is obtained, the actual estimate of S_d for a future period is then readily obtainable because estimates of gross investment for the future—not more distant than the target period—are available from the estimation function for investment.

We can now turn to the net component of savings S_n. In the majority of developing countries, government savings—that is, the excess of government revenues over expenditures—play an important role, and consequently must be introduced as one of the aggregates entering S_n. There is a wide variety of specific forms that the government savings function can assume, depending on availability of statistical information, the actual fiscal structure of each particular country, and other factors. Each particular case calls for its own solution. Let it only be noted that both government current revenues and government current expenditures can generally be linked in some way to the predetermined sectoral value-added variables (the V_j's). For example, corporate income tax revenues can be explained through the value-added in the sectors where the corporate form of organization is predominant. In the developing countries these sectors are typically mining, manufacturing, and in some cases transportation and public utilities.

Another important component of net savings is most often corporate savings (i.e., retained profits). These then can be related to the values-added in the corporate sectors just mentioned. Sometimes, in order to minimize errors which could arise from changes in the corporation tax rates during the period of observation or prediction, it is preferable to construct a single savings relation for gross corporate savings, including corporate taxes, and to take the corporate tax component out of the savings function of the government. This approach was found useful in our case-study for Colombia. In any case, it is highly desirable to treat corporate savings in the aggregate savings function as a separate component because as a general rule this savings relation is the most dynamic vehicle of savings formation in developing countries and as such should not be lumped together with the rest of net private (or nongovernment) savings.

Direct information on savings of households in developing countries is generally inadequate. At this level of economic analysis, however, one has to be content with what data are offered and use them in estimating the corresponding savings relation. In most cases one can hardly do better than relate such savings to total national income of the developing country; in any case, this is a function in which one can have only very little confidence, deviations of actual annual observations from a predicted (fitted) pattern often being enormous. Without going into any detail, let it only be noted that these deviations can sometimes be explained, both statistically and theoretically, through variations in the terms of trade of the developing country or some other measure of relative international values. A good deal of attention is paid to this explanation in this study (see in particular Chapters 3 and 7), and a further outline of the problem is presented in the following section.

The import function

In predicting the future level of imports of developing countries, the first distinction that must be made is that between visible and invisible imports.   Within the latter category, moreover, the line must be drawn between current servicing (not amortization) of debt incurred prior to and during the prediction period on the one hand and all remaining invisible imports on the other.   We can thus write

$$M = M_v + M_{iv}{}^s + M_{iv}{}^{ns} \tag{1-8}$$

where M stands for imports, v for visible, iv for invisible, s for current debt servicing, and ns for other than current debt servicing.   The term $M_{iv}{}^s$ does not call for independent statistical estimation; it can be calculated from balance of payments estimates for the projection period, data on debt incurred in the past, and various assumptions regarding the rate of interest and the amortization schedules.   This is further discussed in the following section; the method is shown in full and applied in Part 2.

Thus we are left with the terms M_v, the visible imports, and $M_{iv}{}^{ns}$, the current invisible imports other than income from foreign debt, to be estimated through statistical methods.   The first of the two, clearly, is the more important, and consequently we shall devote to it most of our discussion.   As for investment, two major avenues of approach are available: one can decompose total goods imports either by economic sector of destination or by physical nature of the imports.   Only rarely can a satisfactory matching between imports and individual sectors of economic activity be obtained for the developing countries.   For example, it is usually difficult to say whether a piece of raw steel goes into the manufacturing, mining, construction, or transportation sector.   Only a careful input-output tabulation—a rare bird in the case of the developing countries—can provide such information.

Thus generally a more promising approach is a disaggregation of imports by type of product, for which detailed information usually is obtainable from the trade returns of developing countries.   Moreover, the economic forces acting on different categories of import products—specifically, capital goods, raw and semifinished products, and consumer goods—are quite different; consequently, this disaggregation can very well be defended on theoretical grounds.

When adopting the second approach (disaggregation by type of product), the sectoral breakdown on the side of the explanatory variables, that is, the breakdown into sectors of economic activity, still remains essential to us in designing the import relations for prediction.   This is so because for many categories of imports it is possible to establish a link with a particular sector of economic activity, or a combination of sectors. The best example here is transportation equipment, whose imports can be directly associated with the value-added in the transportation sector. Alternatively, in the import function for raw materials the value-added in the manufacturing sector can be used as an explanatory variable. Generally it is only for the relatively less important category (in developing countries) of consumer goods that such a sectoral matching cannot be obtained, and the best hypothesis then remains to explain imports of such goods as a function of total national income or product.

Of paramount importance in designing the import estimation function is taking into account the process of import substitution. We have already mentioned this problem in respect to investment and imports of machinery. Suppose that the estimate of investment in machinery has already been obtained for the projection period (see the second alternative in our discussion of the investment function above). An estimate of imports (or net imports in the rare cases where the developing country exports machinery) for the projection period can obviously be obtained by deducting from the investment estimate an estimate of the output of the machinery-producing sector. But the value-added in the machinery-producing sector is one of the basic independent variables of the projection structure V_j. And thus, the only additional component that must be provided to obtain an estimate of imports of machinery is the relation between the value-added and the value of product in the machinery-producing sector. It so happens that this relation is generally found to be quite stable over time not only for one developing country but even among developing countries.

The treatment of import substitution for the category of current inputs —that is, inputs other than capital goods—is usually a good deal more difficult and less satisfactory, at least within the simple projection structure we have adopted. Without going into any detail, let us point out that if import substitution can be handled at all in estimating future imports of current inputs, it can be done only implicitly, by studying variations of import coefficients in the past and by assuming that observed trends, if any, will be continued into the future.

Let us now consider briefly the term M_{iv}^{ns}, that is, the imports of invisibles other than those incurred on account of servicing of outstanding foreign debt. Here data availability generally permits of very little refinement. Fortunately, in total imports this term is rarely important for developing countries. Most often one is satisfied by linking the major categories entering M_{iv}^{ns} to other variables entering the projection structure, such as total national income or total visible imports (this is often a good hypothesis for imports of transportation services).

The export function

As we pointed out when discussing the basic schema earlier in this section, the relation between exports of developing countries and the development process is far less clear-cut than that between development and the other three key aggregates S, I, and M. The important factor causing this difficulty is the influence of foreign demand for exports. Not only does demand for a single developing country's exports depend on incomes and a score of influential policy factors in advanced countries but also it is heavily affected by export supplies in other developing countries.   In the light of these and other complexities, it is extremely difficult, if not impossible, to design a projection structure for exports of individual developing countries which would not make its author blush for shame.   Nonetheless, if we want to obtain estimates of foreign resource requirements, such primitive approaches must, willy-nilly, be attempted.

The corresponding tools, then, are extrapolation of past trends for individual categories of exports, possibly coupled (especially for primary products) with checks of consistency against estimates for total world demand expansion;[5] simple linking of export volume with the growth of export-producing sectors, if identifiable; use of indications in national development plans, and other methods.   Of great importance in respect to exports of primary commodities is the introduction into the export equation of an index reflecting relative prices of such products in the world markets.   This is nothing but taking into consideration the well-known terms-of-trade argument so often made regarding the export earnings of developing countries.

In the final analysis, some comfort can again be derived from the fact that the main purpose of the entire estimation procedure discussed here is not to produce a single (point) estimate of foreign resource requirements of a developing country, but rather to provide a tool for studying the implications of various alternatives.   Among these alternatives, then, we find various postulated rates of expansion of different components of exports, various assumptions regarding future development of the terms of trade, and so forth.

1-3   THE THEORETICAL AND METHODOLOGICAL SIGNIFICANCE OF THE STUDY

As pointed out in section 1-1, our analysis of and work with the Colombian case have led to several theoretical and methodological by-products.   Almost without exception, these by-products are relevant for studies of developing countries similar to that undertaken here for Colombia, as well as for a better general understanding of the development process.   To make these findings accessible to the interested reader, this section is devoted to an outline and a brief discussion of the more important ones.

[5] Such estimates are available for most commodities.

1. Next to the basic estimation procedure discussed in detail in the preceding section, another simple procedure was employed in estimating future foreign resource requirements. In countries heavily dependent on a net inflow of foreign funds over extended periods, servicing of debt incurred in the past can become an important component of gross and net foreign resource requirements in a current period. To make it possible to examine such effects in quantitative terms, a simple estimation procedure was designed; it is presented in section 3-6. It permits the computation of gross and net foreign borrowing and of total debt outstanding in a future period from data, such as the debt in the base period, average interest rate on foreign debt, the projected balance of payments of goods and services excluding interest on foreign debt, the grace period granted to the borrower (if any), and the amortization schedules of past and future debt.

The importance of debt service in total foreign resource requirements is illustrated, on alternative assumptions, by the tabulations of our key estimates in Chapter 4. Although all the calculations leading to those results were performed within two or three man-days using a desk calculator, the equations of section 3-6 can readily be translated into an electronic computer program, which of course leads to the desired results within seconds.[6]

2. As explained in the preceding section, our key estimates of future foreign resource requirements of Colombia depend on a large number (about 50) of estimated or assumed parameters, each of which is unavoidably subject to a possible error. If an error is present, then also the estimate of foreign resource requirements must be biased. Under these conditions, two relevant questions can be asked: (a) What is the probability distribution of each parameter? (b) How does a given change in a parameter from its actual estimated value affect the foreign resource gap estimate?

Not much can be done in respect to answering the first question. The method of deriving each particular parameter in most cases did not permit computation of standard errors. And even if such statistics were obtainable from historical data, there is no reason to believe that in 10 or 15 years—periods for which the key estimates were produced—they would have any real significance.

The second question can quite easily be answered if we use the estimation procedure. Chapter 5 is devoted to this problem. For a selected key estimate, corresponding to what we may call "median" conditions (key estimate A-1), we have performed an analysis of the sensitivity of

---

[6] A somewhat more general program, including as a special case that needed to handle the equations used in this study, has been designed by Dr. Joel Bergsman of the Agency for International Development.

the resource requirement estimates with respect to changes in individual parameters. Our sensitivity index is actually an elasticity—we refer to it later as the *elasticity of transformation*. It is defined, for the six main aggregates to be predicted, as the per cent change in (*a*) exports, (*b*) imports, (*c*) savings, (*d*) investment, (*e*) the savings-investment gap, and (*f*) the export-import gap, corresponding to a 1 per cent change in a given parameter.[7] These calculations were done for all (about fifty) parameters for the projection years 1970 and 1975.

The elasticities of transformation are actually useful in two respects. First, they answer for the researcher or user of the estimates the initial question of how sensitive the gap projections are to changes in structural parameters. Second, they make it possible to directly evaluate alternative estimates of future resource requirements, lest at a later stage a better estimate of a particular parameter is found that is different from that initially used.

3. But there is another possible application of the sensitivity analysis, which the author considers a good deal more important than the two just noted. It can provide us with—at least partial—guidance regarding efficient allocation of scarce foreign resources. Among the many parameters for which transformation elasticities were calculated, rates of growth of eight major sectors of the Colombian economy are included. The transformation elasticities for these parameters, then, show the effect of an increase in the rate of growth of an individual sector on foreign resource requirements in the projection period. If the effect of an increase in a sectoral rate of growth on total national income is ascertained (this is done through another easily computable elasticity index), the impact on total national income (in the projection period) of a dollar of foreign resources—corresponding to each economic sector—can be traced. For example, it may be found that if $1 million of additional foreign resources is used in augmenting the rate of growth of sector i, national product in the projection year will increase by 1 per cent; but if growth in sector j is promoted through the same additional resources, only a $\frac{1}{2}$ per cent increase in national product can be secured.

Such indices, presented also in Chapter 5, actually reflect both the scarce-resource-absorbing and the scarce-resource-augmenting capabilities of individual sectors. Indeed, they are much cruder indicators of efficiency of resource allocation than the theoretically neat shadow prices; however, they are considerably more operational in view of the

[7] It may be useful to give an example: Suppose that the key estimate for the export-import gap for 1975 is $200 million, and the elasticity of transformation between the export price of coffee and the export-import gap is −0.8. Now if the 1975 coffee prices were 10 per cent higher than those assumed in the key estimate ($200 million), it follows that the gap would be 10% × (−0.8) = 8% lower; that is, $184 million.

extremely poor statistical information we have for most less developed countries.

4. The method of evaluating both the (*ex ante*) export-import gap and the (*ex ante*) savings-investment gap is outlined and discussed in the preceding section in technical terms, and corresponding sets of key estimates are produced in Chapter 4. This approach, however, raises a number of conceptual and theoretical problems calling for a comparatively abstract treatment, not entirely dissimilar from the familiar Keynesian analysis, of adjustment from *ex ante* to *ex post* situations wherein both gaps must be equal to each other and also to the volume of inflow (outflow) of resources from (to) abroad.

These questions are treated in Chapter 3. The first two important subjects are (*a*) the identification of the gaps representing the *minimum* foreign resource requirements *consistent* with a prescribed (or postulated) growth rate and sectoral development structure and (*b*) the identification of the dominant minimum gap and analysis of the mechanism whereby the two gaps eventually (and necessarily) come to equality.

5. It is clear that government policies can fully determine, or at least influence, the two types of adjustment—from consistent requirements to minimum consistent requirements and of one gap to the other (dominant) gap. Alternatively, in the absence of any policy action, autonomous economic forces will always perform the adjustment. Certain courses of policy action—or inaction—will then turn out to be more desirable than others from the policy maker's point of view. Moreover, it can be shown, thanks to the dual-gap procedure, that some independent policies (i.e., policies neither related to nor called for by the gap adjustment) may turn out to be quite detrimental to the development process.

6. Although most of the dual-gap analysis, both quantitative and theoretical, is conducted here in respect to situations occurring at some future date, it was possible to design and identify some more or less reliable indicators of actual (historical) gap dominance (see section 6-3). It is such information that may then, in conjunction with the analysis outlined under (5), lead to useful policy recommendations or to the avoidance of policies which would be undesirable.

7. There is another important subject deriving from the economic analysis of the foreign resource gap, perhaps least directly related to the immediate subject of this book, but certainly of great importance for the theory of balance of payments adjustments and, more specifically, for the theory of foreign exchange markets. If there is such a thing as a minimum consistent foreign resource gap, then something in the standing theory of foreign exchanges must give way. Specifically, with appropriate qualifications, there can be no equilibrium whatsoever in the

foreign exchange market corresponding to current transactions. And this then calls for a reconciliation with the accepted economic doctrine. Also, such situations, when and if they arise, will have an important bearing on the criteria for efficient resource allocation, as well as on the criteria to be used in appraising the merits of possible devaluation or appreciation of currency. The subject, in some respects reminiscent of the discussion of the dollar shortage after World War II, is so broad that only an outline of it can be presented here in section 6-4.

8. Under (2) above we dealt with the problem of uncertainty about the future values of structural, as well as other, parameters underlying the projection structure and with the possibility of bias in the foreign-resource-requirements estimates. One such source of bias became quite clearly apparent in the course of preparation of this study, and moreover, we realized that the direction of that bias is not entirely random, but rather predictable, depending on some other parameters of the forecasting model. The parameters subject to such a bias are all the gross capital-output coefficients.

As is shown in greater detail in Chapter 7, the gross marginal capital-output coefficients cannot be expected to be invariant with respect to the rate of growth of the sector whose gross capital formation they are called on to predict. Rather, with increasing rates of growth the coefficients are liable to decline, and with declining rates of growth to increase. The simplest way of explaining it is to point out an extreme situation: with a zero rate of growth of a given production aggregate, the gross capital-output coefficient can be expected to become infinitely large.

It then becomes apparent that if the rate of growth assumed to be realized in the future is significantly different from the rate during the period for which the coefficient was estimated, use of a constant (estimated) gross capital-output coefficient to predict future investment must involve a bias. Not only—as is implicit from the above—is the direction of such a bias predictable but so is the magnitude of the bias, at least as an approximation. Specifically, indices of bias (or distortion) of investment estimates can be computed from data that can be ascertained at least approximately, and such indices then can be used in adjusting the key estimates obtained through the basic procedure (discussed in section 1-2). The equations defining such correction indices are derived in Chapter 7, and the indices are tabulated for some selected values of the determining parameters in the same chapter. These results are then used in Chapter 9, where some final and corrected estimates of future foreign resource requirements of Colombia are derived.

9. As a part of our study of the capital-output coefficient, we have also explored the influence on that coefficient of (a) a scarce labor force and (b) autonomous technical change. Although we did not find it desirable

to include these two factors in the estimation procedure, we discuss the problem briefly in Chapter 7, and treat it rigorously, within the framework of modern growth theory, in the appendix to that chapter.

10. Among the four principal aggregates used in defining the foreign resource gaps, estimation of future savings presented perhaps the greatest difficulties. To a large extent this was caused by the fact that none of the existing theories of saving—whether the Keynesian, or that based on the so-called permanent-income hypothesis, or that based on the so-called relative-income hypothesis—is really adequate to explain the phenomenon of savings in many, if not most, less developed countries. The specific inadequacy found for Colombia, and subsequently in studies of other developing countries undertaken by research groups in the Agency for International Development, is the fact that aggregate savings vary entirely differently with respect to national income, depending on whether changes in income are caused by terms of trade fluctuations or, alternatively, by other causes. The econometric results supporting this statement are presented in section 3-2.

The author's initial incapacity to explain this phenomenon, and the absence (to his knowledge) of a satisfactory explanation in economic literature, led him to a theoretical examination of the problem. The analysis is presented in Chapter 8. Although not as complete and rigorous as it possibly could be, it seems to provide satisfactory answers. For the analysis itself the reader is advised to turn to the relevant sections of this study; however, one general conclusion ought to be stated at this point. If national savings in developing countries undergo rather violent changes as a result of variations in the terms of trade, this is very much a technical necessity inherent in the early process of development and certainly not a result of inadequate management of the growing economies. If, then, in the absence of compensating foreign resource inflow the process of development is impeded as a consequence of unfavorable or declining terms of trade, this is something largely beyond the control of the developing countries themselves.

Chapter 2 THE INITIAL CONDITIONS: COLOMBIA

The main purpose of this chapter is to familiarize the reader with Colombia's historical data for variables which play a central role in our estimation procedure. These variables can be classified into two categories: (1) variables that are taken in the procedure as exogenous, or predetermined, and (2) variables that are to be determined. Within the first category the most important set of data is the gross domestic product and its distribution by sectors of economic activity. These data are presented in Table 2-1. Within the second category we find investment, savings, exports, imports, and information regarding foreign indebtedness and debt servicing. Table 2-2 contains information regarding the balance of payments and external debt. Table 2-3 is a summary of past trends of aggregates entering Colombia's investment and savings.

Before we turn to the individual tables and some of the detail they contain, it is desirable to summarize in a few words the most basic economic data for Colombia. In 1960, the base period of our estimation procedure, Colombia's gross domestic product at factor cost was about 25 billion pesos, that is, at the then prevalent rate of exchange, about US$3.5 billion. Given the population of Colombia, this corresponds to somewhat more than $200 of gross domestic product per capita and around $200 of net national income per capita. While in the three-year period from 1958 to 1961 total real product was increasing at a rate of over 5 per cent, that rate was a good deal lower for the entire decade preceding our base period. Gross investment in 1960 was about 20 per cent of gross

Table 2-1. Colombia—Initial Conditions

Total and Sectoral Gross Value-added (Gross Domestic Product at Factor Cost)

(Values in billions of pesos)

	V Gross domestic product	V_1 Agriculture	V_2 Mining	V_3 Capital goods production	V_4 Other manufacturing	V_5 Construction	V_6 Electricity, gas, water	V_7 Transportation and communication	V_8 All other sectors
Value-added, annual averages:									
1959–1961 at 1960 prices	24.87	8.66	.95	.284†	4.06†	.97	.222	1.57	8.26
1954–1956 at 1960 prices	20.42	7.21	.73	.098†	3.05†	.91	.136	1.38	6.91
1959–1961 at current prices	25.00	8.66	.93	.271	3.86	.96	.221	1.60	8.49
1954–1956 at current prices	12.65	4.81	.29	.059‡	1.84‡	.48	.096	.94	4.13
Real rate of growth:									
1954–1956 to 1959–1961	4.02	3.8	5.4	24	5.9	1.3	10.3	2.6	3.6
1958–1961	5.27	3.1	4.0	15.2	6.2	5.9	10.6	8.2	6.3
Implicit price deflator,									
1954–1956 to 1959–1961	162.3	149.9	246.5	158.5	157.6	187.6	141.1	149.6	172.1

† Implicit price deflators for total manufacturing used since separate figures unavailable.

‡ Figures for 1954–1956 interpolated from (available) figures for 1953 and 1956.

Sources: For all statistics through 1960 except capital goods, UN, *Growth of World Industry, 1938–1961*, p. 157. For 1961 statistics, Departamento Administrativo Nacional de Estadistica, *Anuario General de Estadistica, 1961*, Bogota, Colombia, 1963, p. 477.

For all capital goods statistics, *ibid.*, p. 775.

domestic product, 14 per cent of that investment having been financed through a deficit on current account, and the rest from domestic net savings and depreciation.   In the same year Colombia's imports of goods and services were 27 per cent of the gross domestic product, and exports 24 per cent.   These proportions, primarily owing to wide fluctuations in export earnings, were subject to a considerable degree of change during the 1950s.

To eliminate at least some year-to-year irregularities, three-year averages were computed for the exogenous variables, that is, for the total and sectoral values-added.   The most recent period for which such an average could be obtained is 1959–1961.   Corresponding data are recorded in the first row of Table 2-1; these data are expressed in billions of pesos, at prices of 1960.   They constitute the base for the projections of future income levels and hence for all our estimates of the dependent variables. The table also shows aggregates for the period 1954–1956 in both current and constant prices, aggregates for the base period in current prices, and the implied real rates of growth and price deflators.   A marked difference between economic growth in the second half of the 1950s and the most recently observed growth trends leads us to the computation of real rates of growth between 1958 and 1961.

Of interest is the relatively small size of the power sector (sector 6) and of the capital-goods-producing sector (sector 3).   In the base period each of these sectors accounted for only about 1 per cent of gross domestic product.   However, these two sectors were the fastest growing of all the sectors.   The variation of price trends around the average (162 per cent for the base period with 1954–1956 = 100) is quite pronounced, the lowest implied rate of (factor-) price increase being 41 per cent for public utilities (sector 6), and the highest 147 per cent for the mining industry.

Unfortunately, as is apparent from Table 2-1, it was impossible to identify the services sector, other than transportation.   However, in order to obtain at least a rough impression of the importance of that sector, let it be noted that sector 8, that is, "all other sectors," is primarily imputable to service activities, public and private.   And thus, counting also the transportation sector, we can conclude that in the beginning of the 1960s about 35 to 40 per cent of Colombia's national income was derived from services.

The balance of payments and public foreign debt data are presented in Table 2-2 in millions of U.S. dollars, for the period 1954–1962.   The volatility of export earnings, primarily imputable to drastic terms of trade variations, is probably the most striking characteristic of the balance of payments situation.   Total credits on current account are also heavily influenced by terms of trade changes, but the overall trend is

Table 2-2. Colombia—Initial Conditions

The Balance of Payments on Current Account, Public Debt, and Direct Investment
(Millions of U.S. dollars)

Series description	1954	1955	1956	1957	1958	1959	1960	1961	1962†	1963
Exports f.o.b.‡	$669	$593	$668	$601	$539	$528	$495	$477	$492	
Imports f.o.b.	622	622	605	451	384	403	496	531	516	
Services:										
Credits	29	41	59	79	75	83	96	102	103	
Debits	136	155	136	151	172	148	180	190	201	
Investment income	15	22	16	26	62	38	42	51	55	
Direct investment¶	8	15	11	24	48	19	27	36	33	
Other	7	7	5	2	14	19	15	15	22	
Other services	121	133	120	125	110	110	138	139	146	
Goods and Services:										
Credits	699	634	727	680	614	610	592	578	594	
Debits	758	777	742	602	556	550	676	721	717	
Other current account (net, credits +)	−2	2	2	2	5	2	6	9	3	
Current account (net, credits +)	−62	−141	−13	81	63	63	−79	−134	−120	
Public debt:										
December 31										
Debt outstanding, December 31		276	287	449	459	395	377	466	639	715§
Interest			9	9	14	18	14	14	18	23
Amortization			31	63	112	112	68	61	48	82
Implicit new gross public borrowing			35	231	123	48	50	150	220	
Direct Investment (net, credits +)¶	15	0	10	4	−1	1	3	1	15	

† Provisional data from *Balance of Payments Yearbook*, vol. 15, July, 1963.
‡ Including nonmonetary gold.
§ Recorded June 30, 1963.
¶ Does not include retained unrepatriated earnings.
Source: Except elsewhere specified, International Monetary Fund, *Balance of Payments Yearbook*, vol. 14, December, 1962, Table II; prior to 1957, *Anuario General de Estadística, 1961*, p. 480.

Table 2-3. Colombia—Initial Conditions

Composition of Gross Domestic Investment According to Type of Capital Goods and Source of Financing
(In billions of 1960 pesos)

	1952	1953	1954	1955	1956	1957	1958	1959	1960	1961
Gross domestic investment in fixed capital	3.40	4.60	5.35	5.66	5.37	4.03	3.83	4.11	4.83	5.22
Buildings	.99	1.19	1.46	1.36	1.16	1.13	1.12	1.35	1.25	1.35
Other construction	1.03	1.24	1.62	1.90	1.53	1.43	1.29	1.39	1.45	1.62
Transport equipment	.34	.64	.67	.70	.62	.20	.29	.40	.65	.69
Machinery equipment	1.04	1.53	1.59	1.69	2.06	1.27	1.13	.97	1.42	1.56
Changes in inventories	.34	−.27	−.02	−.01	.29	1.13	.62	.58	.65	.82
Gross domestic investment	3.74	4.23	5.33	5.65	5.66	5.16	4.25	4.69	5.48	6.04
Financing of gross capital formation, per cent†	100	100	100	100	100	100	100	100	100	100
Corporate savings	6	7	8	7	9	9	12	14	14	2
Household savings	17	20	21	17	34	28	1	9	0	10
Government savings	28	26	27	26	23	21	26	28	23	17
Deficit on current account	6	4	6	12	−5	−4	−2	−8	14	17
Depreciation allowances	43	43	38	38	39	46	63	57	49	44

† Computed from data in *Anuario General de Estadistica, 1961*, p. 476.
Sources: 1952–1955, *Anuario General de Estadistica, 1961*, pp. 478–479, investment by type of asset, deflated by implicit deflator for total investment.
1956–1961, UN, *Yearbook of National Accounts Statistics*, 1963.

somewhat less pronounced owing to rapidly growing earnings from services. Public and publicly guaranteed debt—the principal source of long-range deficit financing in Colombia—did not increase significantly through the end of the 1950s because in that period imports of goods and services were at least approximately adjusted through government action. Starting with 1960, however, imports of goods and services expanded a good deal without a corresponding increase in export earnings, and consequently the balance of payments turned from positive to negative, and substantial increases in public debt took place. For a country where a substantial proportion of corporate ownership is foreign and where that ownership was increasing rapidly, a relatively low inflow of foreign direct investment is rather surprising. As can be calculated from the last line of Table 2-2, that inflow was only about $5 million annually on the average over the nine years from 1954 to 1962.

Finally, let us turn to Table 2-3, showing the composition and sources of financing of gross domestic investment. Unfortunately it was impossible to obtain a breakdown of capital formation for the eight sectors of economic activity shown in Table 2-1. Instead, data on distribution of total capital formation are recorded in the table by major physical asset categories. All the investment data are expressed in billions of 1960 pesos.

Of interest is the cycle in total investment. As is apparent from the data on inventory investment, this cycle would be even more pronounced if only fixed asset formation were considered. Recalling the fluctuation in export earnings, and recalling that this fluctuation was strongly determined by terms of trade fluctuations, we can hardly doubt that foreign balance conditions, especially the terms of trade, influence internal capital formation in Colombia, and hence the country's economic progress. This interdependence is especially marked over the first seven years of the period recorded. Thereafter, in spite of export earnings and terms of trade being at a comparatively low level, the volume of fixed capital formation again reveals a favorable trend. The comparatively high rate of economic expansion in the most recent years recorded (see Table 2-2) can be associated with the increasing volume of fixed investment.

The last five lines of Table 2-3 show the principal sources of financing as percentages of total gross capital formation. The percentages were calculated from current peso values. With the exception of corporate savings—the aggregate revealing a strong upward trend—the various individual sources of investment funds fluctuate in a rather erratic fashion. This is especially true in the case of household savings. In fact, the observed patterns of savings by categories cast some doubt about the accuracy of the data, if not about the accuracy of total savings recordings, at least about the distribution of the total.

PART **2** THE ESTIMATION STRUCTURE AND
PROJECTIONS FOR COLOMBIA

Chapter **3** THE STRUCTURE

3-1 INTRODUCTION

The procedure we shall follow in evaluating future aid requirements of Colombia is basically the same as that explained in section 1-2. Consequently, it is unnecessary to reiterate the general considerations which led to that procedure or to state the estimation equations in general terms. Rather, we shall consider the various functions underlying future gap estimates in the remaining sections of this chapter and discuss their respective forms and the methods used in estimating the parameters entering these functions.

As indicated in Chapter 1, the principal exogenous variables whereon the future gap estimates are postulated to depend are the sectoral gross values-added $V_i(i = 1, 2, \ldots, 8)$, adding up to the gross national product at factor cost V; that is,

$$V = \sum_{i=1}^{8} V_i \qquad (3\text{-}1)$$

Identification of the eight sectors is as follows:

$i = 1$	Agriculture
$i = 2$	Mining
$i = 3$	Capital goods manufacturing
$i = 4$	Noncapital goods manufacturing
$i = 5$	Construction
$i = 6$	Electricity, gas, and water
$i = 7$	Transportation and communication
$i = 8$	All other

3-2 THE SAVINGS FUNCTION

For the purpose of the Colombia study we have adopted valuation of both savings and investment on gross rather than on net basis. In other words, savings include capital consumption allowances, and investment refers to formation of all physical assets, including both replacements and new additions to capacity. Not only are these definitions preferable because they make it possible to avoid certain conceptual difficulties—especially that of measuring capital consumption—but in the specific case of Colombia they fit the method adopted and available data better than valuation on a net basis.

Although the exogenous values-added aggregates V_i are valued at factor cost, both savings and investment are valued at market prices. This inconsistency is unavoidable, given conventional national income statistics, and in fact it is not very serious because nowhere in our estimation procedure do the two sets of statistics have to be reconciled with one another. It is postulated only that the latter depend in a specified fashion on the former.

Another point concerning definitions ought to be made before we turn to the discussion of the savings function. The concept of savings we are using here pertains to national rather than domestic savings. In other words, savings are defined as the difference between gross national product (at market prices) and consumption, and they include, among other things, net income of primary factors from abroad. It is the difference between total investment and *national* savings that equals identically, *ex post*, the balance of payments on current account.

Although the effort we expended in considering various forms of the savings function for Colombia was quite considerable, the function we have finally adopted is relatively simple. Total national gross savings S are taken to be the sum of the provisions for consumption of fixed capital S_d (d standing for depreciation), corporate savings and taxes S_{cp}, and a combination of government and household savings, excluding corporate taxes, S_{gh}; that is,

$$S = S_d + S_{cp} + S_{gh} \tag{3-2}$$

For savings on account of depreciation—a substantial part of gross domestic capital formation—we have made an attempt to find the explanation in past gross capital formation. A correlation coefficient between S_d and gross capital formation four years before, significantly higher than for any other time lag, was found. However, the fit between the two variables assuming a four-year time lag was quite unsatisfactory, and therefore this explanation of depreciation allowances was rejected.

A far better result was obtained through a regression of S_d on a moving average of past investments, the a priori hypothesis being that the actual capital consumption and/or write-off pattern is influenced by gross investments over a number of preceding years.   Five-year moving averages of gross fixed investment $\bar{I}^5$, recorded for the third year of the average, are plotted in Figure 2 as a solid line.   Also shown in the diagram are

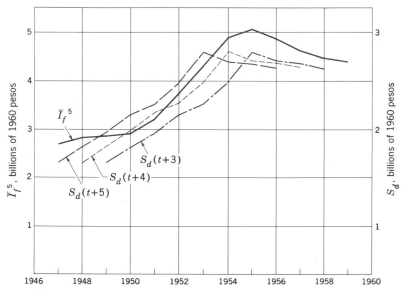

Note: $\bar{I}_f^5$ = gross domestic fixed investment, five-year moving average
$S_d(t+i)$ = savings from depreciation, lagged i years
The years indicated on the time (horizontal) axis refer to $\bar{I}_f^5$. Hence, for example, $S_d(t+3)$ in 1958 will be recorded in the chart for 1955.

Figure 2.   Colombia: Relation between depreciation and fixed investment.

three lines reflecting depreciation allowances S_d moved five, four, and three years respectively backward, measured from the year of actual occurrence.   It is immediately apparent that the three-year lag provides by far the optimal fit.

The resulting function is

$$S = 0.46\bar{I}_{-3}^5 + 0.43 \tag{3-3}$$

where the subscript indicates a three-year time lag for the center of the five-year period.   About 93 per cent of variation in S_d is explained through this equation; moreover, the constant on the right-hand side

(0.43 billion pesos) is relatively unimportant compared to the other term (about 2 billion pesos in 1960).

The next component of the savings function is corporate savings and taxes S_{cp}. A predominant part of the corporate sector in Colombia is composed of mining and manufacturing, that is, our sectors 2, 3, and 4. A comparison of corporate savings and taxes with total value-added of these sectors over the past decade indicates a somewhat faster, but decelerating, growth of the former statistic. Because the relevant proportion has reached a comparatively high level and also because of the observed deceleration, it was decided not to carry into the future the comparatively faster rate of S_{cp} with respect to V_{234}; rather, we use the highest proportion of S_{cp} in value-added, observed in the most recent past. This proportion is 24 per cent, and consequently, as an explanation of corporate taxes and savings, we use

$$S_{cp} = 0.24V_{234} \tag{3-4}$$

Total savings by the households and the government are by far the most important component of *net* savings in Colombia. Both sectors, but especially household savings, reveal an irregular pattern over the past 10 years, average propensity to save of the two sectors taken together ranging between about 0.05 and 0.11. Moreover, any positive dependence of the average propensity on real income cannot be detected. Rather, there is an inverse relation between the two magnitudes on account of another explanatory factor which has varied inversely with the level of real income. As Figure 3 suggests, that factor is the terms-of-trade ratio. In periods when the terms of trade were high, the government and households were able to save a good deal; and in periods of losses of foreign exchange from the terms of trade, the opposite was the case. Using a similar set of hypotheses to those underlying the terms-of-trade explanation, we tried to introduce export earnings as an explanatory variable instead of the terms of trade; but the fit obtained from that relation was a good deal inferior.

The line fitted to the points in Figure 3 yields the following savings function:

$$S_{gh} = V(0.095T - 0.0238) \tag{3-5}$$

where T stands for a terms-of-trade index with 1958 = 1.00; a later revision of savings data for the early 1950s used for relation (3-5) leads to a similar equation,

$$S_{gh} = V(0.073T - 0.0017) \tag{3-6}$$

Functions similar to those just discussed, expanded to include real income as an additional variable, were explored to establish whether there

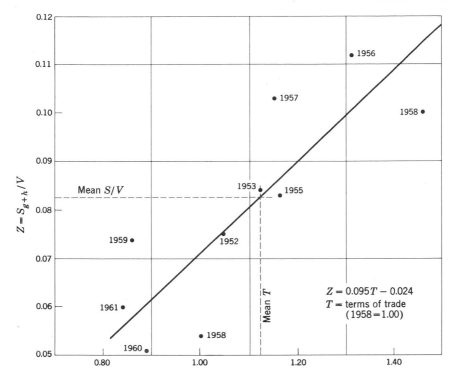

Figure 3.   Colombia: Savings by government and households and the terms of trade.

was a significant difference between marginal and average savings rates for government and households combined. The income coefficient was found extremely small and statistically highly insignificant.

The preliminary results obtained on the impact of the terms of trade on savings led us to a more careful analysis of government and household savings. First of all—as already indicated—the government income from corporate taxes was taken out from government savings, and being much more closely related to corporate profits, it was aggregated with corporate savings [see relation (3-4)]. The rest of government and household savings S_{gh} we took as consisting of the following aggregates:

G = current government expenditure
T_{yp} = direct income and property taxes other than corporate
S_{gh}^* = household savings and indirect taxes combined

that is,

$$S_{gh} = S_{gh}^* + T_{yp} - G \qquad (3\text{-}7)$$

Current government spending measured as a share of national product V has been comparatively stable over the past 10 years and does not reveal any significant trend.   Consequently the average observed over the past decade was used, yielding

$$G = 0.079V \tag{3-8}$$

Noncorporate direct taxes (primarily personal income and property) reveal a definitely faster rate of increase over the past decade than total income.   This is primarily the consequence of a faster-than-average growth of taxable incomes, of improved collection techniques, and more recently of changes in the tax rates.   The observed average rate of growth of T_{yp} exceeds that of total gross factor income by 15 per cent, so that the function we have adopted becomes

$$T_{yp} = \bar{T}_{yp}(1 + 1.15r_V)^t \tag{3-9}$$

where t is time measured from the base period and r_V is the rate of

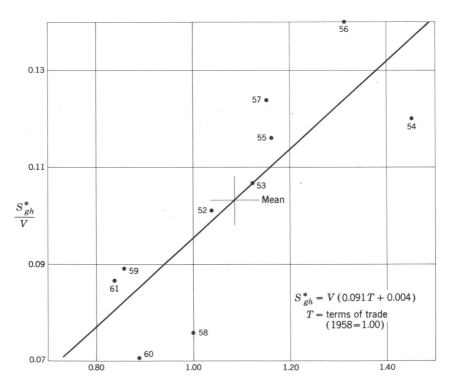

Figure 4.   Proportion of indirect taxes and household savings in national product and the terms of trade.

growth of total national income; the bar on top is used to indicate value in the base period.

The remaining component of S_{gh}, namely S_{gh}^*, deserves attention. The combination of private noncorporate savings and indirect taxes is an aggregate most notably affected by terms-of-trade variations. The share of the variable in national product V is plotted against the terms of trade in Figure 4. The equation of the line fitted to these points is

$$S_{gh}^* = V(0.091T + 0.004) \qquad\qquad (3\text{-}10)$$

where T represents the terms of trade with $1958 = 1.00$. The coefficient of T is about 4.3 times its standard error.

It is interesting to observe that given the order of magnitude of savings and exports in Colombia in the base period 1959–1961 according to relation (3-10), somewhat more than one-half of the loss in foreign earnings on account of a decline in the terms of trade is translated into a decline in savings. This decline is then further translated into a decline in investment and/or an increase in the inflow of foreign resources. It appears from Figure 5 that in the early years of declining terms of trade, that is, in the years immediately following 1954, investment bore most

Figure 5.   Fixed investment and the terms of trade.

of the burden of adjustment, whereas in more recent years the volume of investment has been increasing together with rapidly growing foreign indebtedness.

The observed pattern of Colombian savings is quite consistent with institutional and economic factors. Corporation savings and taxes do not reveal any dependence on the terms of trade; indeed, either the corporate sector is directed toward domestic markets or, to the extent that it is oriented toward exports (e.g., the oil industry), it does not suffer from any significant declines in unit values. On the other hand, significant declines in world prices of the principal export, coffee, and some other exports have directly influenced noncorporate private incomes and hence savings. This direct effect has been accompanied—either via tax receipts or via internal price stabilization schemes for principal export crops—by a reduction of government savings.

The three components of gross national savings discussed thus far and their respective forms [relations (3-3), (3-4), and (3-7)] determine the savings function we use for Colombia. However, before concluding this section it seems desirable to discuss one other hypothesis which was explored. It is the hypothesis that monetary expansion—both inflationary and that called for by real growth—leads to, or is accompanied by, forced savings.

With an observed velocity of monetary circulation of about 5 and an average expansion in money value of national income over the past decade of about 12 per cent, the maximum level of forced savings is about 2.4 per cent of national income. This maximum level would be approximately attained if government current income and expenditure were perfectly exogenous, independent of credit creation, and all monetary expansion took the form of sales of government securities to the central bank, the corresponding proceeds being used to finance investment projects; moreover, the private savers and investors would have to remain unaffected by either inflation or the investment activities of the government.

Aggregating all net savings for Colombia and adding to the terms-of-trade variable (already discussed) the annual rate of change in money income as an additional explanatory variable, we find that the 12 per cent rate of annual expansion observed in the past contributes to savings about 1.6 rather than the hypothetical maximum 2.4 per cent of national income. However, the standard error of the coefficient whereon this result is based is very large, considerably higher than the coefficient itself. Consequently, we have decided not to use the growth in money income as an explanation of savings. We only retain the notion that there is a presumption that internal credit and money expansion contributes to the average propensity to save.

3-3 THE INVESTMENT FUNCTION

Initially an attempt was made to estimate two investment functions, one explaining gross investment, the other net investment. However, the latter alternative was subsequently rejected because for other than the manufacturing sectors it was impossible to obtain satisfactory data for net capital formation.

Using the following notation:

I = gross domestic investment
I_f = gross domestic fixed investment
I_b = investment in buildings (residential and plant)
I_c = investment in other construction (mostly public works)
I_{tr} = investment in transportation equipment
I_m = investment in machinery and equipment
I_v = investment in inventories

our (gross) investment function can be written as

$$I = I_b + I_c + I_{tr} + I_m + I_v \tag{3-11}$$

The choice of the various components entering the investment function was decided by data availability; the five types of investment can be found in the Colombian National Income Accounts in current prices, and they are recomputed at constant prices by the UN Statistical Division (see the UN *Yearbook of National Accounts Statistics*, 1963).

Investment in buildings was taken as depending on total national income V in a linear fashion. For investment in plant, the less important component of the aggregate, this may not be the most realistic assumption; an acceleration relationship might have been a better hypothesis. However, it was impossible to explore this approach, for lack of separate data on plant construction. For the rest of the aggregate a linear relation appears preferable to an accelerator because investment in housing often is a reflection of savings (in kind) rather than of a derived demand for capital goods by an economic sector. Not having any information on sectoral investment in buildings, we have assumed that this investment is related to all factor income. The function derived is

$$I = 0.053V \tag{3-12}$$

The coefficient is computed as the average propensity to invest in buildings over the three-year base period 1959–1961. It compares quite satisfactorily with that computed for the three-year period 1954–1956, namely, 0.057.

Of similar form is the investment function for inventory formation,

$$I_v = 0.021V \tag{3-13}$$

This rather unsophisticated function is as good a result as can be obtained. In a number of primary-product-exporting countries, inventory investment is dominated by forces other than those usually identified in advanced countries. Year-to-year changes of inventories in Colombia reveal an extremely erratic pattern over the past 10 years. To eliminate such short-run disturbances and record the central tendency of the statistic, we have derived our coefficient as an average over the 10-year period 1952–1961.

The remaining three components of the investment function are all based on the acceleration hypothesis. In other words, it is postulated that demand for machinery, transport equipment, and construction other than buildings depends on the rate of growth of the using sectors. Using subscripts to indicate sectors (more than one subscript represents the relevant variable pertaining to the sectors indicated) and letting r stand for the rate of growth, we can write the gross investment function for machinery and equipment as

$$I_m = 3.33 r_{23456} \bar{V}_{23456}(1 + r_{23456})^t \tag{3-14}$$

where the bar on top of V indicates the base period (average value-added, at constant prices of 1960, over the three-year period 1959–1961) and t represents the projection date measured from zero in the base period.

Not having any information on use of machinery in the different sectors, we have related total demand for such capital goods to the rate of growth of the principal machinery-using sectors, that is, mining, manufacturing, construction, and power. The coefficient 3.33 is computed from the observed rate of growth of the combined value-added sector between 1958 and 1961 and the average demand for machinery and equipment over the base period. It would have been preferable to use value-added data for a somewhat later period to allow for gestation, but this was impossible to do because no information for the years after 1961 was available. A partial check of accuracy of the coefficient was made by computing that same coefficient on data for 1953–1956; it came out within 20 per cent above the figure appearing in relation (3-14). The lower coefficient derived from most recent data was used because there are reasons to believe that the other reflects less accurately the true value of the capital-output coefficient.

Assuming that construction other than buildings depends primarily on the growth of sectors appearing in the above equation (sectors 2 through 6) and on the transportation sector (sector 7), the following demand function for gross investment in construction other than buildings is obtained:

$$I_c = 2.90 r_{234567} \bar{V}_{234567}(1 + r_{234567})^t \tag{3-15}$$

In this particular instance the coefficient 2.90 is obtained as an average of coefficients computed for the base period and for 1954–1956 respectively, the range of the two coefficients being just about 10 per cent.

A good deal of difficulty was encountered in estimating the investment function for transportation equipment. Coefficients computed for the two periods already indicated give widely different results. Lumpiness of transportation projects and excess capacity operation in some periods are probably the most important explanations of this irregularity. To eliminate as much as possible the short-run disturbances, we have calculated our capital-output ratio for transportation from the entire sample of historical data available, that is, from 1952 to 1961. The resulting function is as follows:

$$I_{tr} = 7.71 r_7 \bar{V}_7 (1 + r_7)^t \tag{3-16}$$

3-4 THE EXPORT FUNCTION

Far less than the other three key aggregates—savings, investment, and imports—do exports of Colombia depend on domestic conditions. In a number of respects foreign demand is the prevalent factor. This basic fact is reflected in the export function for Colombia. It also renders the export function considerably less reliable compared with the other behavioral relations we are using.

The export function is relatively simple because in the particular case of Colombia two products, coffee and petroleum, represent well over 80 per cent of the value of visible exports. Using the following set of notations:

E = exports of goods and services (f.o.b.)
E_c = exports of coffee
E_p = exports of petroleum
E_o = other visible exports
E_s = exports of services
$P_c{}^t$ = price index of coffee at time t, base period = 1.00
$P_p{}^t$ = price index of petroleum at time t, base period = 1.00
r_c = rate of growth of Colombia's exports of coffee
r_o, r_s = defined similarly
$\bar{E}_c$ = exports of coffee in base period (1959–1961 average)
$\bar{E}_p, \bar{E}_o, \bar{E}_s$ = defined similarly
X_p = domestic production of petroleum
C_p = domestic consumption of petroleum
η = income elasticity of demand for petroleum in Colombia

the total export function can be expressed as

$$E = E_c + E_p + E_o + E_s \tag{3-17}$$

Exports of coffee, the first term on the right-hand side of relation (3-17), can be explained for a future period t (measured from zero in the base year) as

$$E_c = P_c{}^t \bar{E}_c (1 + r_c)^t \tag{3-18}$$

$\bar{E}_c$ is an observed number, while the price index and the real rate of growth are parameters, depending primarily on foreign economic conditions, which cannot be derived as part of the estimation procedure. Rather, we use estimates obtained by other authors. The alternative values of r_c and $P_c{}^t$ actually used are given and further discussed in Chapter 4 when we come to the key alternative estimates.

Because Colombia is both an important user and a net exporter of petroleum and petroleum products, an attempt was made to reflect in our estimates of oil exports conditions of both domestic supply and domestic demand. To do this, we postulated that net exports of petroleum are the difference between domestic output and domestic consumption of petroleum. Using data for consumption observed over the past 10 years, we estimated η, the income elasticity of demand for petroleum and petroleum products, as 2.27. The resulting export function for petroleum then becomes, in billion of pesos,

$$E_p = P_p{}^t \left[\bar{E}_p + 0.016 \left(\Delta X_p - 2.27 \frac{\Delta V}{V} \bar{C}_p + \Delta M_p \right) \right] \tag{3-19}$$

where the bar on top again indicates the base period and ΔM_p is the change in imports of fuels (predominantly petroleum products) measured in millions of barrels. It will be observed that all the magnitudes in the inner bracket on the right-hand side of relation (3-19) are expressed in millions of barrels and that the coefficient .016 is price per million barrels in billions of pesos. The change in volume of imports is derived from the import function, discussed in the following section. All terms on the right-hand side of relation (3-19) are thus known except for the price index $P_p{}^t$ and the change in output of petroleum ΔX_p. Whereas the former magnitude is assumed to be equal to 1 for all our estimates of future exports (thus it is useful for only the sensitivity analysis), crude information on ΔX_p, at least through 1970, can be obtained from exploration data and plans for future oil field expansion. According to the International Bank for Reconstruction and Development, it can be expected that output will increase in 1965 by 38 per cent, and in 1970 by 68 per cent as compared with the base period. These data also include the effect of an expected improvement in internal pipeline facilities. The IBRD experts indicate that at present exports are about 20 per cent lower than they could be in the absence of internal oil transportation bottlenecks.

The remaining two components of exports, that is, visible exports (other than oil and coffee) and exports of services, are both relatively unimportant in the base period. However, both of these export aggregates grew comparatively fast in the past, the first at about 7.5 per cent, the second at about 14 per cent per annum. Although promotion of non-primary exports in Colombia makes it a plausible assumption that the former rate will continue into the future, it seems highly unlikely, judging from the structure of the expansion, that this will be the case for the latter rate. It is thus assumed that services earnings will expand in the future only at one-half the rate observed in recent past, that is, 7 per cent per annum.

The export function for other exports thus can be written as

$$E_o = \bar{E}_o(1 + r_o)^t \qquad\qquad (3\text{-}20)$$

and the export function for services

$$E_s = \bar{E}_s(1 + r_s)^t \qquad\qquad (3\text{-}21)$$

Only in the context of the sensitivity analysis presented in Chapter 5 are the two rates of growth to be understood as variable. All the key estimates (see Chapter 4) are based on the assumptions that $r_o = 0.074$ and $r_s = 0.070$.

3-5   THE IMPORT FUNCTION

Because financing of balance of payments deficits, and hence considerations regarding debt, amortization, etc., enters explicitly the estimation procedure (see the following section), the import function we are using for Colombia excludes interest on public debt. This magnitude can be estimated only after balance of payments data are available, that is, using information concerning both exports and imports. Thus, with the exception of interest on public debt, the import function is designed to explain all imports on current account. Visible imports are valued c.i.f.

Imports on current account M, including interest on public debt, are explained as a sum of imports of raw material M_r, imports of fuels M_f, imports of transportation equipment M_{tr}, imports of other capital goods (primarily machinery) M_m, imports of base metals M_{bm}, all other visible imports M_o, imports of services other than income from direct investment M_{s1}, and income from direct investment M_{s2}. Thus we have

$$M = M_r + M_f + M_{tr} + M_m + M_{bm} + M_o + M_{s1} + M_{s2} \qquad (3\text{-}22)$$

Imports of raw materials were studied over the past 10 years in relation to value-added of the two raw-material-using sectors, that is, V_{34}.

Whereas significant fluctuations from year to year have occurred in the past (especially in 1958), no trend whatsoever is noticeable in the ratio of the two variables. This merely indicates that in spite of an effort for import substitution a relatively rapid growth of the material-using sectors did not permit a reduction of the materials-import coefficient. Only the structure of materials imports has changed considerably. It is assumed that the pattern of the past will continue into the future and that the coefficient observed over the 10-year period 1952–1961 can be used to explain imports of raw materials, that is,

$$M_r = 0.062V_{34} \tag{3-23}$$

A similar examination of past behavior of imports of fuels in relation to value-added in the principal using sectors (manufacturing, transportation, and power) reveals a declining import coefficient. Expansion of domestic output of petroleum and of refining capacity is consistent with that trend (note that virtually all imports of fuels into Colombia are imports of petroleum products). Because the most recently observed import coefficient is very small and, for lack of ability to predict its changes in the future, we use that coefficient to explain future imports of fuels into Colombia, we have

$$M_f = 0.016V_{3467} \tag{3-24}$$

Actually, stability of that coefficient in the future is quite plausible—in spite of expected expansions of refining capacity—because of a relatively high income elasticity of demand for petroleum and petroleum products in Colombia. Recall from the preceding section that the elasticity is estimated at 2.27.

On the assumption that Colombia will not become an important exporter of transportation equipment in the foreseeable future, we can explain imports of transportation equipment as the difference between total demand for, and domestic output of, such capital assets. Since the former magnitude, that is, total demand, is derived as part of the investment function (see section 3-3), only future output of transportation equipment in Colombia must be estimated to obtain the import function. There is fairly stable relationship between total output of the Colombian transportation equipment industry X_{tr} and the value-added in that sector $V_3{}^{tr}$. In the base period 1959–1961 the average relation comes out to $X_{tr} = 1.94V_3{}^{tr}$. And thus the import function for transportation equipment can be written as

$$M_{tr} = 7.71r_7(1 + r_7)^t \bar{V}_7 - 1.94(1 + r_3{}^{tr})^t \bar{V}_3{}^{tr} \tag{3-25}$$

Using the investment function for machinery and equipment and using an analogous procedure to that just gone through for transportation equipment, we obtain the corresponding import function. It will be observed that here the principal using sectors are sectors 2 to 6. The relation between domestic output of machinery X_m and value-added in that sector is $X_3{}^m = 2.25V_m$. The complete import function is

$$M_m = 3.33r_{23456}(1 + r_{23456})t\bar{V}_{23456} - 2.25(1 + r_3{}^m)^t\bar{V}_3{}^m \tag{3-26}$$

where r, as in our previous relationship, represents the rate of growth; the subscript 3 stands for the particular sector, i.e., production of capital goods; and the superscript m indicates the subsector of sector 3, machinery.

The principal importers of base metals in Colombia are manufacturing, our sectors 3 and 4, and construction, sector 5. The import function for these semimanufactures has been constructed similarly to the import function of raw materials. In both cases, no trend in the import coefficient is observable. The average coefficient derived for the base period is used here to obtain the following explanation of imports of base metals:

$$M_{bm} = 0.057V_{345} \tag{3-27}$$

Other imports, including primarily consumer goods but also nonconsumer chemical products, can most conveniently be explained as depending on total national income V. A stable relation between national income and other imports over the past 10 years leads to the function,

$$M_o = 0.052V \tag{3-28}$$

However, because the growth of the Colombian economy is least vulnerable to variations in this aggregate, it can be expected that the observed average propensity to import 0.052 could change (in either direction) in the future as a consequence of deliberate changes in commercial policy. Thus, while we invariably use relation (3-28) in our key projections (see Chapter 4), the more significant results derivable from that relation appear in Chapter 5, where we study the sensitivity of the gap estimates to changes in parameters. In fact, the most natural interpretation of the average propensity to import "other" products is to take that magnitude as a policy parameter.

Imports of services other than earnings on foreign investment—not including shipping and insurance charges because visible imports are valued c.i.f.—have been increasing in the past at a relatively slow rate, about $\frac{1}{4}$ of that of real national income. Because this aggregate is composed of a large number of unimportant and rather dissimilar types of expenditures, some of which cannot even be exactly identified, we must be content with assuming for this type of imports the low income elasticity of demand implied by the proportion just mentioned. Thus we have

$$M_{s1} = \bar{M}_{s1}(1 + \tfrac{1}{4}rv)^t \tag{3-29}$$

Perhaps the most difficult to estimate among the import aggregates are the earnings of foreign direct investment. The highly irregular pattern of that statistic over the past 10 years recalls only one other series that we have been considering in the present procedure—that of the investment in inventories. A similar procedure was adopted here to eliminate as much as possible the extreme short-run variations. We have postulated that, on the whole, earnings on foreign direct investment will depend on the net worth (that is, assets minus liabilities) of foreign corporations in Colombia W. The long-run average relation between W and M_{s2} is

$$M_{s2} = 0.114W \tag{3-30}$$

Relation (3-24) is also our import function for M_{s2}. It is remarkable that in spite of virtually zero net inflow of foreign direct funds into Colombia during the past decade, W has been expanding quite fast, a good deal faster than can be explained by a revaluation of real assets in an inflationary economy. It can be concluded that the residual expansion can be attributed to retained, unrepatriated earnings.

Because there is a very heavy concentration of foreign direct investment in petroleum production in Colombia, we make the assumption that W will be expanding in the future *pari passu* with petroleum output. This assumption then provides us with the magnitudes of W to be substituted into relation (3-30).

Before we conclude our discussion of the import function, a few words must be said regarding commercial policy. Except in connection with other imports M_o, considerations of commercial policy did not enter the derivation of the import function. Now it is clear that, for example, a 300 per cent tariff on any category of imports would have a considerable impact on the import function. And consequently the absence of commercial policy parameters from our function must be explained.

It will be recalled that our principal aim is the estimation of foreign resource requirements for economic development, the increments in and structure of national product being the predetermined set of data for which foreign resource requirements are to be found. Suppose now that a 300 per cent duty is introduced on imports of machinery. If a parameter reflecting such a policy does not appear in the import function, it is not that we would consider the effects of duties negligible, but rather that, if the 300 per cent levy reduced the volume of machinery imports by, say, 50 per cent, the rate and structure of development postulated at the outset could not be attained, and thus the very assumptions whereon the estimation procedure is based would be vitiated.

A whole score of important theoretical and conceptual issues lies behind what has just been said; we shall return to these issues in Chapter 6. At this stage of the argument it is necessary only to raise the question of commercial policy—and in fact of many other types of policy—in connection with our estimation procedure.

3-6 DEBT SERVICE AND THE BALANCE OF PAYMENTS

It will be recalled from the preceding section that our import function represents imports on current account excluding interest on public and publicly guaranteed debt. Consequently, the balance of payments estimates—to be referred to hereafter as B^*—that can be derived from the export and import functions obtained thus far also exclude interest on debt. But it is B^* plus interest on debt outstanding that equals total balance of payments on current account B, and the latter, in turn, determines net additions to indebtedness. Net additions to indebtedness plus debt at the end of the preceding year, finally, determine total debt outstanding at the end of the current year.

It follows that the total balance of payments on current account B cannot be estimated for a future date unless the relationships just outlined are systematically carried out for the whole period between the base year and the projection year. Using available information on Colombian present public debt and our estimates of B^* obtained through the procedures explained in the preceding two sections, we make an attempt to estimate the total balance of payments for selected future years. We do so using alternative sets of assumptions concerning the rate of interest, the amortization periods, and the so-called grace periods, that is, periods when temporarily no amortization of loans is required.

This analysis has two very important by-products: (1) estimates of total debt outstanding at a future date D_t and (2) estimates of gross public capital flow requirements G_t. The second type of estimates especially can be very valuable; in some situations G_t is a better index of a country's international payments position than the balance of payments on current account B.

Stated formally, the procedure is as follows:

Given:

1. B_t^*, deficit in the balance of payments on current account excluding interest on public debt in period t
2. D_0, the debt outstanding in period zero (that period can be different from the base period used in the preceding sections)

3. a_t,   amortization payment on initial debt D_0 in period t
4. v_t,   total interest payment on the portion of D_0 (after amortization) still outstanding at the beginning of period t
5. i,   average rate of interest on all new debt outstanding, that is, debt contracted from period 1 on, minus all amortization of that debt to date
6. k,   average amortization period of new debt, counted from the end of the grace period
7. g,   the grace period

Calculate for the projection period (base through 1970 or 1975):

8. B_t,   deficit in the balance on current account in year t
9. A_t,   all amortization payments in year t
10. G_t,   gross inflow of public funds in year t
11. D_t,   total public debt outstanding at the end of year t

Assuming that there will be no net flow of other than public or publicly guaranteed funds in the future, we can obtain the results from the following equations:

$$D_t = D_{t-1} + B_t \tag{3-31}$$
$$G_t = B_t + A_t \tag{3-32}$$
$$B_t = B_t^* + v_t + i\left(D_{t-1} - D_0 + \sum_{p=1}^{t-1} a_p\right) \tag{3-33}$$

and finally

$$A_t = a_t + \frac{1}{k} \sum_{p=1}^{t-1} G_p f_p \tag{3-34}$$

with

$$f_p = 1 \quad \text{for } p < t - g$$
$$f_p = 0 \quad \text{for } p \geq t - g$$

This procedure is based on the assumption of no direct investment flow, that is, $d_t = 0$. If $d_t \neq 0$ ($d_t > 0$ representing capital inflow in period t) the above procedure can easily be amended in the following way. Observe that

$$B_t = B_t^* + M_t{}^i = d_t + D_t - D_{t-1} \tag{3-35}$$

where $M_t{}^i$ is all interest payments on public debt in period t. Consequently

$$B_t - d_t = (B_t^* - d_t) + M_t{}^i = D_t - D_{t-1} \tag{3-36}$$

Now letting B_t stand for $(B_t - d_t)$ and B^* stand for $(B_t^* - d_t)$, the above procedure can be used without alteration in calculating D_t and G_t. The true balance on current account then can be obtained from relation (3-36).

Of course, d_t must be estimated and becomes an additional exogenous variable.

While B^* is estimated as part of the procedure explained in the preceding sections, data listed under (2) to (4) above, that is, data regarding the initial debt position, have been obtained for Colombia from an IBRD compilation and are reproduced in Table 3-1 in millions of U.S. dollars.

Table 3-1

		Total payments during year		
Year	Initial debt outstanding plus undisbursed January 1†	Amortization (a_t)	Interest (v_t)	Total debt service
1963	\$715.2 $(= D_0)$	\$82.5	\$24.1	\$106.6
1964	698.9	75.0	23.8	99.7
1965	622.0	61.1	23.1	84.2
1966	560.0	44.1	21.9	66.3
1967	514.8	39.5	20.5	59.9
1968	474.6	35.6	18.8	54.4
1969	438.2	28.3	17.3	45.6
1970	409.3	28.2	16.0	44.2
1971	380.6	24.7	14.7	39.4
1972	355.4	24.3	13.6	37.9
1973	330.7	27.1	12.4	39.6
1974	303.2	27.9	11.2	39.1
1975	275.0	28.6	9.9	38.6
1976	246.0	28.4	8.6	37.0
1977	217.4	25.5	7.1	32.6

† Data in this column show the (initial) debt as recorded in 1963 and, for subsequent years, the remainder of that debt after annual amortization payments.   The amounts recorded for 1965, 1970, and 1975 are a portion of *total* debt in those years, estimated in the following chapter using the basic gap estimates B^* and the procedure presented in this section.

The other data, listed under (5) to (7) above are parameters that cannot be exactly known, but whose approximate values can be either estimated from past experience or taken as policy parameters subject to decisions by the lending countries.   In computing our gap estimates (see Chapter 4) we assign these parameters various "realistic" values and estimate the corresponding alternative magnitudes of B, D, and G.

Of course, it is desirable to evaluate all the magnitudes sought in dollars rather than in domestic currency.   For this it is necessary to have all the data entering the procedure, that is, B_t^*, D_0, a_t, and v_t, given in dollars.   Whereas data on initial public debt (such as those in Table 3-1) are generally given in dollars, the estimates of B^* may not be.   If the estimates of B^* are valued in terms of domestic currency, they must be converted to dollars, using the exchange rate of the base period.   If a single rate of exchange is applicable, that rate can be applied directly to estimates of B^* in domestic currency.   If multiple exchange rates are applicable, these ought to be used in converting the various components entering B^*.   In the calculations for Colombia presented in the following chapter, two "average" rates, slightly different from each other, are used for exports and imports respectively.

3-7   SUMMARY OF THE ESTIMATION FUNCTIONS

The principal purpose of this section is to present in a compact fashion the various estimation functions derived and explained in sections 3-1 to 3-5.   The procedure relating to debt and debt servicing is not reiterated in this section and thus must be studied from section 3-6.

A secondary purpose of this section is to state all the functions, as far as possible, in terms of initial (base-period) values and of assumed rates of growth.   Consequently, some of the functions stated below are written differently from the way they were stated in the foregoing sections.   Using base-period data (always indicated with a bar on top) and rates of growth has two important analytical advantages: (1) The base period can be shifted at will to produce other estimates later, assuming the basic structure remains unchanged; (2) this formulation is much more advantageous in calculating partial derivatives of the gaps and, from those, the transformation elasticities underlying the sensitivity analysis (Chapter 5).

GENERAL OBSERVATIONS AND NOTATIONS

V = gross domestic product at factor cost = ΣV_i, $i = 1, 2, \ldots, 8$, where V_i = value-added in sector i.   Sectors: (1) agriculture; (2) mining; (3) capital goods manufacturing; (4) noncapital goods manufacturing; (5) construction; (6) electricity, gas, and water; (7) transportation and communication; (8) all others.

r_{ij} = rate of growth of sectors i and j taken together.   A bar on top of a variable indicates an average taken over the base period 1959–1961.

The numerical coefficients and parameters in the following functions are assumed constant in the key estimates in Chapter 4.

Savings:

$$S = S_d + S^*_{gh} + P_c + T_{yp} - G$$

Savings from deprecia-
tion:

$$S_d = 0.46\bar{I}_{-3}{}^5 + 0.43$$

Savings by households
and indirect govern-
ment taxes:

$$S^*_{gh} = (0.091T + 0.004)\bar{V}(1 + r_v)^t$$

Corporate profits (cor-
porate savings
+ corporate taxes):

$$P_c = 0.24\bar{V}_{234}(1 + r_{234})^t$$

Personal income taxes
and property taxes:

$$T_{yp} = \bar{T}_{yp}(1 + 1.15r_v)^t$$

Government spending
on current account:

$$G = 0.079\bar{V}(1 + r_v)^t$$

$\bar{I}_{-3}{}^5 =$ gross domestic fixed investment, five-year moving average, lagged three years

$T =$ terms of trade (1958 = 1.00)

Investment:

$$I = I_b + I_c + I_m + I_{tr} + I_v$$

Investment in build-
ings:

$$I_b = 0.053\bar{V}(1 + r_v)^t$$

Investment in other
construction:

$$I_c = 2.90r_{234567}\bar{V}_{234567}(1 + r_{234567})^t$$

Investment in machin-
ery and equipment:

$$I_m = 3.33r_{23456}\bar{V}_{23456}(1 + r_{23456})^t$$

Investment in trans-
portation equip-
ment:

$$I_{tr} = 7.71r_7\bar{V}_7(1 + r_7)^t$$

Investment in inven-
tories:

$$I_v = 0.021\bar{V}(1 + r_V)^t$$

Exports of goods
and services (f.o.b.):

$$E = E_c + E_p + E_o + E_s$$

Exports of coffee:

$$E_c = P_c{}^t\bar{E}_c(1 + r_c)^t$$

Exports of petroleum:

$$E_p = P_p{}^t\left[\bar{E}_p + 0.016\left(\Delta X_p - 2.27\frac{\Delta V}{V}26.1 + \Delta M_f\right)\right]$$

Other visible exports:

$$E_o = \bar{E}_o(1 + 0.074)^t$$

Exports of services

$$E_s = \bar{E}_s(1 + 0.07)^t$$

$P_c{}^t$ and $P_p{}^t$ are the price indices of coffee and petroleum respectively at time t (1959–1961 = 1.00); r_c is the rate of growth of the value of Colombia's exports of coffee at base-period world prices; X_p is domestic production of petroleum; and M_f is imports of petroleum and petroleum products, both measured in millions of barrels.

Imports of goods
(c.i.f.) and services:

$$M = M_r + M_f + M_{bm} + M_m + M_{tr} + M_o + M_{s1} + M_{s2}$$

Imports of raw
materials:

$$M_r = 0.062\bar{V}_{34}(1 + r_{34})^t$$

Imports of fuels:

$$M_f = 0.016\bar{V}_{3467}(1 + r_{3467})^t$$

Imports of base
metals:

$$M_{bm} = 0.057\bar{V}_{345}(1 + r_{345})^t$$

Imports of machin-
ery:

$$M_m = 3.33 r_{23456}\bar{V}_{23456}(1 + r_{23456})^t - 2.25 V_3{}^m$$

Imports of transpor-
tation equipment:

$$M_{tr} = 7.71 r_7\bar{V}_7(1 + r_7)^t - 1.94 V_3{}^{tr}$$

Other visible
imports:

$$M_o = 0.052\bar{V}(1 + r_V)^t$$

Imports of services:

$$M_{s1} = \bar{M}_{s1}(1 + 0.25 r_V)^t$$

Net direct invest-
ment income:

$$M_{s2} = 0.114\bar{W}(1 + 0.051)^t$$

$V_3{}^m$ and $V_3{}^{tr}$ are the values-added by domestic production of machinery and transport equipment respectively $(V_3{}^m + V_3{}^{tr} = V_3)$; W is the net worth of foreign enterprises.

Chapter 4 THE KEY ESTIMATES

4-1 A GUIDE TO THE KEY ESTIMATES

In this chapter we employ the estimation structure derived in Chapter 3 in evaluating savings, investment, exports, imports, and the corresponding foreign resource gaps for 1965, 1970, and 1975. In order to describe the spectrum of "possible" alternatives adequately, the author judged it necessary to produce 13 key estimates. To make these results easily accessible and intelligible to the reader, this section provides a guide to the key estimates.

Of all the possible alternative projections for which the estimation structure can be used, only some "key" alternatives are explored here. These alternatives can be classified as follows: (1) alternatives with respect to sectoral rates of growth (and consequently, with respect to the overall growth of the economy), (2) alternatives with respect to certain selected parameters, and (3) alternatives with respect to conditions of public debt servicing. All other alternatives permitted by our specific method—primarily those resulting from variation of parameters—are dealt with in Chapter 5, where we use the method of transformation elasticities.

It cannot be overemphasized here that the alternatives that we can explore cannot be any more refined than the estimation structure from which they are derived. Many alternatives, in fact perhaps the most interesting ones for a developing country, cannot be examined.   Among these are alternatives with respect to investment in training and education.   As it is, in our structure the education sector is lumped together with "all other productive activities" (sector 8), and consequently we cannot even assess its relative importance.   But even if we could, our ignorance of the marginal social product of education would still hamper evaluation of the alternatives with respect to the allocation of resources to education.   The applicability of our procedure is almost equally limited when it comes to the evaluation of alternative government policies, whether in the sphere of credit creation, taxation, or commercial policy.   The only difference is that in these instances, our procedure combined with an additional effort could lead to some reasonably realistic estimates.   Such estimates, however, were deemed beyond the scope and resources of the present study.

Four alternative sectoral growth patterns were studied and are presented in sections 4-2 to 4-5 respectively.   The first (key estimate A) is a median pattern, yielding an overall rate of growth of the economy of about 5 per cent, and is based on sectoral rates projections of the Committee of Nine of the Alliance for Progress.   The second (key estimate B) is a high growth alternative, based on extrapolation of most recent past trends; it corresponds to an overall growth rate of the Colombian economy of about 5.5 per cent.   Next comes a low alternative (key estimate C); it is based primarily on low rates of growth observed over various past periods and corresponds to an overall rate of growth of 4.5 per cent. Finally, key estimate D reflects the sectoral growth assumptions of the Colombia National Development Plan (discussed in greater detail in section 4-5).   Key estimate D is what we may term a very high growth alternative, the rate being about 6 per cent; it is presented here primarily to explore the feasibility of the Development Plan.

Several variants of each of the four key estimates (A, B, C, and D) have been computed, each variant depending on three of the following eight conditions:

1. No change in terms of trade between 1959–1961 and projection years.
2. Terms of trade T improve linearly to the 1958 level by 1970 ($\Delta T = +16.3\%$).
3. Rate of growth of coffee exports 0.028 (Source: B. Balassa).
4. Coffee exports grow at a rate of 0.022 (Source: IBRD).
5. Observed linear growth of capital goods:
   transportation equipment $V_3{}^{tr} = V_3{}^{tr}(1 + 0.125t)$
   machinery $V_3{}^{m} = \bar{V}_3{}^{m}(1 + 0.156t)$
6. Growth of capital goods industries according to UN (Chenery-Edelman) expansion elasticities.   The implicit expansion 1960–1970 is 89 per cent.
7. Exponential growth of capital goods industries:
   transportation equipment   0.10 per annum
   machinery   0.15 per annum

8. Observed exponential growth of capital goods industries (1956–1961):
   transportation equipment   0.12 per annum
   machinery   0.22 per annum

The four major alternatives, A, B, C, and D, with their variants lead to our 13 key estimates. Each of the 13 estimates is presented in a separate table at the end of the relevant section (section 4-2 for estimates A, section 4-3 for estimates B, etc.). Each set of estimates, A, B, C, or D, is preceded by a summary statement of underlying assumptions concerning sectoral rates of growth and the other conditions. The text of the four sections is devoted to the discussion of the assumptions and the analysis of the results.

Using the procedure presented in section 3-6, we evaluate for each of the 13 key estimates the total balance of payments, including interest on public debt, the total debt outstanding, and gross (implied) borrowing of public funds for each of the projection years. We do so under alternative assumptions regarding the average rate of interest on new debt i, the grace period (if any) g, and the average amortization period of new debt k. The results, together with listing of assumed values for the three parameters, are presented in the lower part of each of the key estimate tables.

Because there is no objective basis for converting the domestic aggregates—savings and investment—into foreign currency, we have chosen to present all the major aggregates and the gaps in terms of pesos. Only the export-import gap (excluding interest on public debt) B^* is then recomputed into dollar values, and that figure is then used as a basis for evaluation of the total balance of payments, debt, and gross borrowing in terms of dollars.

The exchange rates used in converting exports and imports into dollar values are 6.71 and 6.91 pesos per dollar respectively. These are the average rates implicit in published peso and dollar values of exports and imports in the base period 1959–1961. If one wants to get an approximate idea of the orders of magnitude of the savings-investment gaps in millions of dollars, it is necessary to multiply the tabulations in billions of pesos by a factor of 150, which is an approximation of one thousand times the inverse of the rates 6.71 and 6.91. Because throughout the estimation we have used values in terms of the base-period prices, all the peso estimates of future gaps are also expressed—with the possible exception of coffee exports noted above—in values at average base-period prices, that is, prices of 1959–1961. Given our procedure of conversion from pesos into dollars, our dollar estimates ought to be understood (except possibly for coffee) as valued at 1959–1961 average dollar prices and exchange rates.

As will be noted from the tables, we make the assumption throughout that all future balance of payments deficits will be financed through increments in public and publicly guaranteed debt.   In other words, net private capital flows (as well as grants) are assumed to be zero in the future.   Judging from past experience, this assumption is quite realistic for direct investment in Colombia.   However, if long-run foreign investment other than increments in public debt were predicted to take place in Colombia, the desired adjustments of the estimates presented here can be obtained using the procedure explained in section 3-6.   An approximate judgment on the effect of other than public capital flows can also be made by comparing the results obtained here for different key estimates.

4-2   KEY ESTIMATES A: COMMITTEE OF NINE SECTORAL RATES OF GROWTH

As indicated in the preceding section, the alternative key estimates A and a summary of the underlying assumptions are presented at the end of this section.   The sectoral rates of growth on which the estimates are based are taken from the Committee of Nine (Alliance for Progress), *Evaluation of the General Economic and Social Development Program of Colombia* (1962), p. 42.   Although these rates pertain only to the period 1959–1965, we have concluded that they represent what could be termed a "central," or median, expectation for sectoral developments in Colombia at least through 1970.

The overall rate of growth of the economy implied by these rates, measured from the base period 1959–1961, is 4.9 per cent through 1965, 5 per cent through 1970, and 5.1 per cent through 1975.   These rates of expansion are somewhat lower than what was experienced in Colombia in the period 1958–1961 and a good deal higher (almost 1 percentage point) than the average rate of growth over the second half of the 1950s.   Also, as will be noted later in this section, the aid levels called for by this alternative are not exorbitant, and under certain favorable conditions to be discussed later, the necessary aid and/or capital flow could become quite small.   The per capita growth rate implied by the assumptions of key estimates A is over 2 per cent.

Next to the sectoral rates of growth the five key estimates presented here are based on sets of alternative assumptions regarding some key parameters.   Alternative assumptions are made about both the export prices of coffee—affecting the terms of trade—and the rate of growth of coffee exports.   Because it is extremely difficult to predict future expansion of capital goods industries, several alternative assumptions were made regarding the growth of this sector, ranging from very high rates (about 19 per cent) observed in the past to low estimates based on the results of a UN study of industrial expansion (see Bibliography).

With the exception of key estimate A-1, all estimates are computed only for the years 1965 and 1970. The reason is that with a horizon further than 10 years from the base period the degree of uncertainty about the true structure to prevail in that period is considerable. Only key estimate A-1 is carried to the year 1975. In part this was done to show the implications of the various assumptions for that period; however, our principal motive was to establish a basis for the sensitivity analysis carried out in Chapter 5.

As indicated on top of the key estimate tables, both dollar and peso valuations are used in presenting the results. Owing to a multiple exchange rate system, there is no single rate of exchange applicable to both exports and imports. The implicit average exchange rate in the base period 1959–1961 is 6.70 pesos per dollar for exports and 6.89 pesos per dollar for imports. Given this situation, there is hardly any objective basis for converting savings and investment figures from domestic currency into dollars. Consequently, we have performed all our calculations in terms of peso values (at constant base-period prices), and all the results of the main part of the estimation procedure are also presented in (billions of) pesos.

For exports and imports (excluding interest on public debt) we have used the implicit exchange rates of the base period in calculating estimates of the balance of payments B^* in (millions of) dollars. In this way it is possible to estimate the total balance of payments B, debt outstanding, and gross borrowing in dollars, using dollar estimates on service of past debt compiled by the IBRD (see section 3-6).

It is thus possible to compare directly the peso estimates of the savings-investment gap with the estimates of B^*—the balance of payments excluding the interest on public debt. To obtain an approximation of the total balance of payments B in pesos, it is necessary to multiply the difference between B and B^* by the import exchange rate of about 7 pesos per dollar and add that product onto the peso estimate of B^*.

Let us now briefly examine the key estimate A-1. This median estimate, characterized by an overall rate of growth of about 5 per cent, does not reveal a very pronounced difference between the foreign exchange gap and the savings-investment gap in 1970, our central projection year. With a deficiency of resources for investment of 2.12 billion pesos in that year, the deficiency of foreign exchange to finance imports is about 2 billion pesos assuming a 5 per cent rate of interest on newly contracted debt (since 1963) and about 1.8 billion assuming a low rate of 3 per cent. Considering the overall accuracy of the estimates, these differences do not appear significant. There is good reason to believe that even if the *ex ante* savings-investment gap were to turn out somewhat larger by 1970, no serious difficulties of *ex post* adjustment could be expected for that period even if only the foreign exchange gap were to be financed through external funds; more will be said about this presumption in Part 3.

Perhaps more interesting is the comparison of the two gaps over time. Using the assumption of a 3 per cent rate of interest on foreign borrowed funds, we find the increases of *IS* and *B* over the three periods studied to be as follows:

	1960–1965	1965–1970	1970–1975
IS	1.98	0.40	0.43
B	1.33	0.82	0.85

Considering that in 1970 the two gaps are about equally important, it follows that the savings-investment constraint would be dominant in the 1960s and the foreign exchange constraint after 1970. In other words, the foreign exchange gap, even though initially smaller, can be expected to grow considerably faster than the savings-investment gap. A similar situation characterizes a number of our key estimates and actually is encountered quite systematically in many other less developed countries. Provided that the government pursues sound budgetary policies over a number of years, the savings constraint is liable to become of secondary importance relative to the foreign exchange constraint. For Colombia, the sensitivity analysis presented in Chapter 5 throws some additional light on this subject.

The estimates of debt service are another subject deserving attention. They are especially revealing for key estimate A-1 because we consider here a 15-year period. By 1975 the interest cost is quite considerable. With a 5 per cent rate of interest on newly contracted debt the deficit on current account is $531 million in that year, with a 3 per cent rate it is $450 million, and with a zero rate it is $354 million, only $10 million greater than B^*. Note that the $10 million is the interest on the remainder of debt outstanding in 1963.

Total debt itself increases at a very high rate over the 12-year period 1963–1975, considerably faster than either national income, exports, imports, or any other major economic indicator. On the assumption of a 3 per cent rate of interest the compound annual rate is 14 per cent, and on the assumption of a 5 per cent rate of interest the growth rate is almost 15 per cent.

As will be observed from the results tabulated in the bottom part of key estimate A-1, conditions of amortization and/or grace period affect only gross borrowing; as could be expected, with a 10-year grace period we obtain the lowest figure for borrowing in 1975: only $86 million above net capital inflow.   The highest figure—again on the assumption of a 3 per cent rate of interest—is obtained for a 15-year average amortization period and no grace period.   That figure is almost $700 million, as compared with $450 million for net capital inflow.

Key estimate A-2 reveals the important role of the terms of trade. Assuming that the terms of trade of Colombia would return to the 1958 level, that is, increase by about 16 per cent from the base period, the foreign exchange gap in 1970 would be reduced by just about one-half, (as compared with the key estimate A-1) on either assumption regarding the rate of interest.   The debt and gross borrowing estimates are correspondingly lower.   Because the terms of trade affect the savings-investment gap considerably less than the foreign exchange gap, the savings-investment gap in this situation (key estimate A-2) definitely becomes dominant, and short-run *ex post* adjustment of one kind or another would have to take place.   But this adjustment will be our concern only later in Part 3.

As shown by key estimate A-3, the foreign exchange gap becomes somewhat greater if the IBRD assumption is used for the expected rate of growth of Colombia's coffee exports.   That rate is 2.2 per cent per annum as compared with the 2.8 per cent used in the first two key estimates.   On this assumption the foreign exchange gap becomes dominant in 1970, with a 5 per cent rate of interest charged on newly contracted debt, and the two gaps are about equal at a little over 2 billion pesos assuming a 3 per cent rate of interest.

One of the most difficult estimates to make is that regarding future rate of growth of capital goods industries.   In the three key estimates considered thus far the assumption made was that the high rates of growth of the capital-goods-producing industries observed in the past will not be continued in the future but rather will be followed by a linear trend. Another possibility is explored in key estimate A-4.   We have used here the rate of expansion of capital goods industries implied by the results of a United Nations study of the expansion elasticities of various industries in developing countries (see Bibliography, No. 14).   Compared with past performance and the assumptions of the preceding three key estimates, this approach yields a rather conservative estimate.   This is then reflected by an increase in the estimate of the foreign exchange gap, an increase resulting from a lesser substitution of domestic capital goods for imports of those goods.

Another variant of key estimate A is presented in key estimate A-5.

In that estimate we assume that capital goods output will keep growing at an exponential rate over the projection period; however, the exponential rates observed in the past are assumed to be reduced in the future from 22 to 15 per cent for machinery and from 12 to 10 per cent for transportation equipment. The key estimate A-5 shows how potent a tool for improving the foreign exchange gap is capital goods import substitution. For example, for 1970 the expected balance of payments deficit with a 3 per cent interest rate is only about $150 million. A comparable figure in key estimate A-1 is $90 million higher.

COLOMBIA: KEY ESTIMATES A

Basic assumptions specification: Committee of Nine sectoral rates of growth

Sectoral Rates of Growth	
Sector	*Rate*
1. Agriculture	0.036
2. Mining	0.065
3. Capital goods	0.064
4. Other manufactures	
5. Power	0.087
6. Construction	0.125
7. Transportation	0.056
8. All others	0.045
Overall	0.050

OTHER ASSUMPTIONS

1. No change in terms of trade between 1959–1961 and projection years.
2. Terms of trade T improve linearly to the 1958 level by 1970 ($\Delta T = +16.3\%$).
3. Rate of growth of coffee exports 0.028 (Source: B. Balassa).
4. Coffee exports grow at a rate of 0.022 (Source: IBRD).
5. Observed linear growth of capital goods:
   transportation equipment $V_3{}^{tr} = \bar{V}_3{}^{tr}(1 + 0.125t)$
   machinery $V_3{}^m = \bar{V}_3{}^m(1 + 0.156t)$
6. Growth of capital goods industries according to UN (Chenery-Edelman) expansion elasticities. The implicit expansion 1960–1970 is 89 per cent.
7. Exponential growth of capital goods industries:
   transportation equipment   0.10
   machinery   0.15

OTHER ASSUMPTIONS IN INDIVIDUAL KEY ESTIMATES

A-1: 1, 3, 5
A-2: 2, 3, 5
A-3: 1, 4, 5
A-4: 1, 3, 6
A-5: 1, 3, 7

Assumptions Regarding Balance of Payments Deficit Financing

Alternative	Grace period g, years	Interest on foreign debt i, %	Amortization period k, years
(a)	0	3	15
(b)	0	5	15
(c)	0	3	25
(d)	10	3	15

Colombia: Key Estimate A-1

(Valuation: constant 1960 prices and exchange rates; billion pesos and million dollars)

Basic assumptions specification: Committee of Nine (Alliance for Progress) sectoral rates; no change in terms of trade; linear growth of capital goods production

Series description	Base period 1959–61	1965	1970	1975
Overall rate of growth of: GNP f.c.	.040†	.049	.050	.051
Investment, gross, pesos	5.40	7.53	10.22	13.98
Savings, national, gross, pesos	4.89	6.01	8.10	10.94
Investment − savings, pesos	0.51	1.52	2.12	3.04
Imports, current account excluding interest on debt, pesos	4.36	5.68	7.30	9.88
Exports, current account, pesos	3.97	4.87	5.89	7.32
Imports − exports = B^*, pesos	0.39	0.81	1.41	2.56
= B^*, dollars	$41	$99	$182	$344

Total balance of payments deficit = B
Assumptions on debt service:‡

		1965	1970	1975
$g = 0, i = 3\%, k = 15$	(a)	$133	$242	$450
$g = 0, i = 5\%, k = 15$	(b)	141	275	531
$g = 0, i = 3\%, k = 25$	(c)	$57	133	242	450
$g = 10, i = 3\%, k = 15$	(d)	133	242	450

Capital flow other than public funds, net		0	0	0

Public debt outstanding, January 1

		1965	1970	1975
	(a)	$930	$1,805	$3,415
	(b)	934	1,871	3,734
	(c)	$715§	930	1,805	3,415
	(d)	930	1,805	3,415

Gross inflow of public funds

		1965	1970	1975
	(a)	$219	$367	$692
	(b)	227	406	795
	(c)	209	328	607
	(d)	194	270	536

† Period: 1954–1956 through 1959–1961.
‡ g = grace period, years
i = interest on foreign debt
k = amortization period, years
§ 1963.

Colombia: Key Estimate A-2

(Valuation: constant 1960 prices and exchange rates; billion pesos and million dollars)

Basic assumptions specification: Committee of Nine sectoral rates; return in terms of trade to 1958 level ($\Delta T/T = .163$) due to increase in world prices during 1960–1970; linear growth of capital goods production

Series description		Base period 1959–1961	1965	1970
Overall rate of growth of: GNP f.c.		.040†	.049	.050
Investment, gross, pesos		5.40	7.53	10.22
Savings, national, gross, pesos		4.89	6.28	8.61
Investment − savings, pesos		0.51	1.25	1.61
Imports, current account excluding interest on debt, pesos		4.36	5.68	7.30
Exports, current account, pesos		3.97	5.16	6.59
Imports − exports = B^*, pesos		0.39	0.52	0.71
= B^*, dollars		$41	$55	$77
Total balance of payments deficit = B Assumptions on debt service:‡				
$g = 0$, $i = 3\%$, $k = 15$	(a)		$87	$124
$g = 0$, $i = 5\%$, $k = 15$	(b)	$57	94	148
$g = 0$, $i = 3\%$, $k = 25$	(c)		87	124
$g = 10$, $i = 3\%$, $k = 15$	(d)		87	124
Capital flow other than public funds, net			0	0
Public debt outstanding, January 1				
	(a)		$869	$1,377
	(b)	$715§	872	1,447
	(c)		869	1,377
	(d)		869	1,377
Gross inflow of public funds				
	(a)		$169	$221
	(b)		176	249
	(c)		160	193
	(d)		143	152

† Period: 1954–1956 through 1959–1961.
‡ g = grace period
  i = interest on foreign debt
  k = amortization period, years
§ 1963.

Colombia: Key Estimate A-3

(Valuation: constant 1960 prices and exchange rates; billion pesos and million dollars)

Basic assumptions specification: Committee of Nine sectoral rates; no change in
terms of trade but using IBRD projections for coffee exports; linear growth
of capital goods production

Series description	Base period 1959–1961	1965	1970
Overall rate of growth of: GNP f.c.	.040†	.049	.050
Investment, gross, pesos	5.40	7.53	10.22
Savings, national, gross, pesos	4.89	6.01	8.10
Investment − savings, pesos	0.51	1.58	2.12
Imports, current account excluding interest on debt, pesos	4.36	5.68	7.30
Exports, current, account, pesos	3.97	4.80	5.72
Imports − exports = B^*, pesos	0.39	.88	1.58
= B^*, dollars	$41	$109	$208

Total balance of payments deficit = B
Assumptions on debt service:‡

		Base period 1959–1961	1965	1970
$g = 0, i = 3\%, k = 15$	(a)		$143	$270
$g = 0, i = 5\%, k = 15$	(b)	$57	150	305
$g = 0, i = 3\%, k = 25$	(c)		143	270
$g = 10, i = 3\%, k = 15$	(d)		143	270

Capital flow other than public funds, net			0	0

Public debt outstanding, January 1

		Base period 1959–1961	1965	1970
	(a)		$944	$1,906
	(b)	$715§	947	1,994
	(c)		944	1,906
	(d)		944	1,906

Gross inflow of public funds

		1965	1970
	(a)	$230	$402
	(b)	236	442
	(c)	220	361
	(d)	206	300

† Period: 1954–1956 through 1959–1961.
‡ g = grace period, years
  i = interest on foreign debt
  k = amortization period, years
§ 1963.

Colombia: Key Estimate A-4

(Valuation: constant 1960 prices and exchange rates; billion pesos and million dollars)

Basic assumptions specification: Committee of Nine sectoral rates; no change in terms of trade; Chenery-UN function for increase in capital goods production

Series description	Base period 1959–1961	1965	1970
Overall rate of growth of: GNP f.c.	.040†	.049	.050
Investment, gross, pesos	5.40	7.53	10.22
Savings, national, gross, pesos	4.89	6.01	8.10
Investment − savings, pesos	0.51	1.52	2.12
Imports, current account excluding interest on debt, pesos	4.36	5.83	7.60
Exports, current account, pesos	3.97	4.87	5.89
Imports − exports = B^*, pesos	0.39	0.96	1.71
= B^*, dollars	$41	$120	$225
Total balance of payments deficit = B Assumptions on debt service:‡			
$g = 0, i = 3\%, k = 15$ (a)		$154	$289
$g = 0, i = 5\%, k = 15$ (b)	$57	161	326
$g = 0, i = 3\%, k = 25$ (c)		154	289
$g = 10, i = 3\%, k = 15$ (d)		154	289
Capital flow other than public funds, net		0	0
Public debt outstanding, January 1			
(a)		$960	$1,996
(b)	$715§	973	2,086
(c)		960	1,996
(d)		960	1,996
Gross inflow of public funds			
(a)		$242	$427
(b)		248	470
(c)		233	383
(d)		218	320

† Period: 1954–1956 through 1959–1961.
‡ g = grace period, years
  i = interest on foreign debt
  k = amortization period, years
§ 1963.

Colombia: Key Estimate A-5

(Valuation: constant 1960 prices and exchange rates; billion pesos and million dollars)

Basic assumptions specification: Committee of Nine sectoral rates; no change in terms of trade; exponential rate of growth of capital goods production

Series description		Base period 1959–1961	1965	1970
Overall rate of growth of: GNP f.c.		.040†	.049	.050
Investment, gross, pesos		5.40	7.53	10.24
Savings, national, gross, pesos		4.89	6.01	8.10
Investment − savings, pesos		0.51	1.52	2.14
Imports, current account excluding interest on debt, pesos		4.36	5.61	6.74
Exports, current account, pesos		3.97	4.87	5.89
Imports − exports = B^*, pesos		0.39	0.74	0.85
= B^*, dollars		$41	$88	$100
Total balance of payments deficit = B Assumptions on debt service:‡				
$g = 0, i = 3\%, k = 15$	(a)		$121	$152
$g = 0, i = 5\%, k = 15$	(b)	$57	128	186
$g = 0, i = 3\%, k = 25$	(c)		121	152
$g = 10, i = 3\%, k = 15$	(d)		121	152
Capital flow other than public funds, net			0	0
Public debt outstanding, January 1				
	(a)		$914	$1,581
	(b)	$715§	917	1,660
	(c)		914	1,581
	(d)		914	1,581
Gross inflow of public funds				
	(a)		$206	$262
	(b)		213	308
	(c)		197	230
	(d)		183	181

† Period: 1954–1956 through 1959–1961.
‡ g = grace period, years
  i = interest on foreign debt
  k = amortization period, years
§ 1963.

4-3   KEY ESTIMATES B: CONTINUATION OF RECENT TRENDS

Whereas key estimates A were designed to study the aid requirements of the Colombian economy under median conditions, the two key estimates B presented in this section correspond to a "high," or "optimistic," development alternative.   The estimates B can be considered realistic— contrary to our "very high" alternative D—in the sense that each of the sectoral rates of growth used in deriving these estimates has been realized in the past.   The overall rate of growth of the economy implied by the sectoral rates used here is about 5.5 per cent for the 1960s.   This overall rate and all the sectoral rates of growth have been realized in the period 1958–1961.   If then the hypothesis of absorption capacity is a correct one, that is, if there is some invariant natural upper limit to the rate of growth at which various productive sectors in developing countries can grow, the basic assumptions of our key estimates B must be realistic. The only limiting condition imposed on the rate of economic development would then be the availability of savings and/or foreign exchange resources.

With the exception of the rates of growth of the various sectors of the Colombian economy, key estimate B-1 is comparable with key estimate A-1.   Specifically, the same assumptions are made here with respect to the terms of trade, the rate of growth of coffee exports, and the rate of growth of capital goods industries as were made for key estimate A-1. The differences between the various numerical estimates are thus entirely imputable to different sectoral growth rates.

The first thing we observe is that the increase from 5 to 5.5 per cent rate of growth of the economy (that is, from the assumptions of key estimate A-1 to those of B-1) leads in 1970 to an increase in foreign exchange requirements of about $150 million, whether we assume a rate of interest on debt of 3 per cent or 5 per cent.   On the latter assumption the difference is somewhat larger.   Correspondingly, public debt in 1970 increases by about $600 million on either assumption.   It is as high as $2.5 billion assuming a 5 per cent rate of interest; this is a 250 per cent increase over the debt level in 1963.

The second fact deserving mention is that with the higher rates of growth underlying the key estimate B-1 the foreign exchange constraint becomes dominant in 1970.   Recalling that the import exchange rate is about 7 pesos per dollar and that the entire difference between B and B^* is imputable to the debit side of the balance of payments, we find from the table that the *ex ante* deficit in the balance of payments for 1970 is about 2.80 billion pesos.   In 1965 the savings-investment gap is the more important of the two, but the difference is reduced as compared with the key estimate A-1.

There are good reasons to believe that if the overall rate of growth of the Colombian economy could be stepped up in the 1960s from 5 to 5.5 per cent, the expansion of the capital goods industries could also be accelerated.   Consequently, in our second key estimate (key estimate B-2) we make. the alternative assumption of an exponential rate of growth for these industries, 15 and 10 per cent per annum for machinery and transportation equipment respectively.   The same assumption is made for key estimate A-5.   Whereas the impact of this alternative assumption on the savings-investment gap is hardly noticeable, it is very important with regard to the foreign exchange gap.   The latter is reduced in 1970 from $384 million (estimate B-1) to $283 million (estimate B-2) assuming a 3 per cent rate of interest on debt.   For a relatively high rate of interest on debt of 5 per cent the corresponding two figures are $431 million and $325 million respectively.

COLOMBIA: KEY ESTIMATES B

Basic assumptions specification: Observed sectoral rates, 1958–1961

Sectoral Rates of Growth	
Sector	*Rate*
1. Agriculture	0.031
2. Mining	0.040
3. Capital goods	0.067
4. Other manufactures	
5. Power	0.059
6. Construction	0.106
7. Transportation	0.082
8. All others	0.063
Overall	0.055

OTHER ASSUMPTIONS

1. No change in terms of trade between 1959–1961 and projection years.
3. Rate of growth of coffee exports 0.028 (Source: B. Balassa).
5. Observed linear growth of capital goods industries:
   transportation equipment $V_3{}^{tr} = \bar{V}_3{}^{tr}(1 + 0.125t)$
   machinery $V_3{}^{m} = \bar{V}_3{}^{m}(1 + 0.156t)$
7. Exponential growth of capital goods industries:
   transportation equipment   0.10
   machinery   0.15

OTHER ASSUMPTIONS IN INDIVIDUAL KEY ESTIMATES

B-1: 1, 3, 5
B-2: 1, 3, 7

Assumptions Regarding Balance of Payments Deficit Financing

Alternative	Grace period g, years	Interest on foreign debt i, %	Amortization period k, years
(a)	0	3	15
(b)	0	5	15
(c)	0	3	25
(d)	10	3	15

Colombia: Key Estimate B-1

(Valuation: constant 1960 prices and exchange rates; billion pesos and million dollars)

Basic assumptions specification: Past trends, 1958–1961, sectoral rates; no change
in terms of trade; linear growth of capital goods production

Series description	Base period 1959–1961	1965	1970
Overall rate of growth of: GNP f.c.	.040†	.055	.055
Investment, gross, pesos	5.40	7.92	10.90
Savings, national, gross, pesos	4.89	6.10	8.38
Investment − savings, pesos	0.51	1.82	2.52
Imports, current account excluding interest on debt, pesos	4.36	6.11	8.08
Exports, current account, pesos	3.97	4.84	5.81
Imports − exports = B^*, pesos	0.39	1.27	2.28
= B^*, dollars	$41	$166	$307

Total balance of payments deficit = B
Assumptions on debt service‡

		Base period 1959–1961	1965	1970
$g = 0, i = 3\%, k = 15$	(a)		$203	$384
$g = 0, i = 5\%, k = 15$	(b)	$57	213	431
$g = 0, i = 3\%, k = 25$	(c)		203	384
$g = 10, i = 3\%, k = 15$	(d)		203	384

		Base period 1959–1961	1965	1970
Capital flow other than public funds, net			0	0

Public debt outstanding, January 1

		Base period 1959–1961	1965	1970
	(a)		$1,027	$2,395
	(b)	$715§	1,031	2,514
	(c)		1,027	2,395
	(d)		1,027	2,395

Gross inflow of public funds

		1965	1970
	(a)	$295	$548
	(b)	306	603
	(c)	283	494
	(d)	264	412

† Period: 1954–1956 through 1959–1961.
‡ g = grace period, years
  i = interest on foreign debt
  k = amortization period, years
§ 1963.

Colombia: Key Estimate B-2

(Valuation: constant 1960 prices and exchange rates; billion pesos and million dollars)

Basic assumptions specification: Past trends, 1958–1961, sectoral rates; no change in terms of trade; exponential growth of capital goods production

Series description		Base period 1959–1961	1965	1970
Overall rate of growth of: GNP f.c.		.040†	.055	.055
Investment, gross, pesos		5.40	7.92	10.92
Savings, national, gross, pesos		4.89	6.10	8.42
Investment − savings, pesos		0.51	1.82	2.50
Imports, current account excluding interest on debt, pesos		4.36	6.04	7.54
Exports, current account, pesos		3.97	4.84	5.81
Imports − exports = B^*, pesos		0.39	1.20	1.73
= B^*, dollars		$41	$156	$228
Total balance of payments deficit = B Assumptions on debt service:‡				
$g = 0, i = 3\%, k = 15$	(a)		$193	$283
$g = 0, i = 5\%, k = 15$	(b)	$57	202	325
$g = 0, i = 3\%, k = 25$	(c)		193	283
$g = 10, i = 3\%, k = 15$	(d)		193	283
Capital flow other than public funds, net			0	0
Public debt outstanding, January 1				
	(a)		$1,013	$2,183
	(b)	$715§	1,017	2,292
	(c)		1,013	2,183
	(d)		1,013	2,183
Gross inflow of public funds				
	(a)		$284	$433
	(b)		294	483
	(c)		272	384
	(d)		254	311

† Period: 1954–1956 through 1959–1961.
‡ g = grace period, years
  i = interest on foreign debt
  k = amortization period, years
§ 1963.

4-4   KEY ESTIMATES C: A LOW GROWTH ALTERNATIVE

We have observed that the overall rate of growth of Colombia in the second half of the 1950s was as low as 4 per cent per annum. Nothing precludes the possibility that such a rate of growth, or only a slightly higher one, could be realized through the 1960s. This possibility would become especially likely if Colombia were to receive during the present decade only a limited amount of foreign aid, or no aid at all. To study the implications of a low growth alternative, we have selected from between the sectoral rates of growth, observed either in the recent past (1958–1961) or in the second half of the 1950s, the lower of the two. Moreover, in one or two cases where the low rate of growth was unrealistically low, we have adjusted it upward, using as an additional piece of information rates assumed by the Committee of Nine (see key estimate A-1).

The average rate of growth for the economy as a whole resulting from these sectoral rates is 4.5 per cent. This rate is $\frac{1}{2}$ per cent below our median alternative (A) and 1 per cent below the high "realistic" alternative (B). As will be apparent from the key estimate C, the 4.5 per cent rate—together with the underlying sectoral mix of rates of growth—is consistent with a self-sustained growth of the Colombian economy, or at least is very close to such a rate. In other words, it can be postulated that the Colombian economy could grow at a rate of 4.5 per cent with no, or only very little, foreign aid. This will be discussed further in Part 3. At this point observe only that such a rate implies in the case of Colombia only about 1.5 per cent annual increment in per capita income.

Only two alternative key estimates C were made: key estimate C-1, based on the same assumptions as A-1 and B-1 except for the sectoral rates of growth, and key estimate C-2, based on the same assumptions as A-1 except for an improvement in the terms of trade by 1970 to the level of 1958. On the assumption that the terms of trade would not improve at all from the base period, the foreign exchange gap in 1970 would be $116 million assuming a 3 per cent rate of interest on foreign debt and $138 million with a high 5 per cent rate. The latter figure just about matches the savings-investment gap. Consequently, with a rate of interest of 3 per cent, the savings constraint would be dominant.

The key estimate C-2 is our only estimate yielding a negative deficit (i.e., surplus) in the balance of payments excluding interest on debt B^*. The total balance of payments B happens to be exactly zero on our low interest rate assumption and is only $12 million when an average rate of 5 per cent is charged on public debt used to finance deficits over the projection period. The savings-investment gaps for 1965 and 1970 are also considerably reduced compared with those in key estimate C-1 and actually are the lowest in all the key estimates. Although the balance of payments, assuming 3 per cent rate of interest on public debt, is zero in 1970, that is, net borrowing is zero, a figure as high as $63 million is estimated for gross borrowing in 1970, on the assumption of a 15-year amortization period and a zero grace period.

COLOMBIA: KEY ESTIMATES C

Basic assumptions specification: Minimum observed sectoral rates (see text for further explanation)

Sectoral Rates of Growth	
Sector	*Rate*
1. Agriculture	0.031
2. Mining	0.040
3. Capital goods	0.059
4. Other manufactures	
5. Power	0.059
6. Construction	0.100
7. Transportation	0.056
8. All others	0.045
Overall	0.045

OTHER ASSUMPTIONS

1. No change in terms of trade between 1959–1961 and projection years.
2. Terms of trade T improve linearly to the 1958 level by 1970 ($\Delta T = +16.3\%$).
3. Rate of growth of coffee exports 0.028 (Source: B. Balassa).
5. Observed linear growth of capital goods industries:
   transportation equipment $V_3{}^{tr} = \bar{V}_3{}^{tr}(1 + 0.125t)$
   machinery $V_3{}^m = \bar{V}_3{}^m(1 + 0.156t)$

OTHER ASSUMPTIONS IN INDIVIDUAL KEY ESTIMATES

C-1: 1, 3, 5
C-2: 2, 3, 5

Assumptions Regarding Balance of Payments Deficit Financing			
Alternative	*Grace period g, years*	*Interest on foreign debt i, %*	*Amortization period k, years*
(a)	0	3	15
(b)	0	5	15
(c)	0	3	25
(d)	10	3	15

Colombia: Key Estimate C-1

(Valuation: constant 1960 prices and exchange rates; billion pesos and million dollars)

Basic assumptions specification: Minimum "observed" trends for sectoral rates; no change in terms of trade; linear growth of capital goods production

Series description		Base period 1959–1961	1965	1970
Overall rate of growth of: GNP f.c.		.040†	.045	.045
Investment, gross, pesos		5.40	6.63	8.60
Savings, national, gross, pesos		4.89	6.06	7.62
Investment − savings, pesos		0.51	0.57	0.98
Imports, current account excluding interest on debt, pesos		4.36	5.30	6.61
Exports, current account, pesos		3.97	4.89	5.95
Imports − exports = B^*, pesos		0.39	0.41	0.66
$= B^*$, dollars		$41	$40	$72
Total balance of payments deficit $= B$ Assumptions on debt service:‡				
$g = 0, i = 3\%, k = 15$	(a)		$72	$116
$g = 0, i = 5\%, k = 15$	(b)	$57	76	138
$g = 0, i = 3\%, k = 25$	(c)		72	116
$g = 10, i = 3\%, k = 15$	(d)		72	116
Capital flow other than public funds, net			0	0
Public debt outstanding, January 1				
	(a)		$847	$1,292
	(b)	$715§	850	1,353
	(c)		847	1,292
	(d)		847	1,292
Gross inflow of public funds				
	(a)		$152	$207
	(b)		177	233
	(c)		145	182
	(d)		133	144

† Period: 1954–1956 through 1959–1961.
‡ g = grace period, years
  i = interest on foreign debt
  k = amortization period, years
§ 1963.

Colombia: Key Estimate C-2

(Valuation: constant 1960 prices and exchange rates; billion pesos and million dollars)

Basic assumptions specification: Minimum "observed" trends for sectoral rates;
return in terms of trade to 1958 level; linear growth
of capital goods production

Series description	Base period 1959–1961	1965	1970
Overall rate of growth of: GNP f.c.	.040†	.045	.045
Investment, gross, pesos	5.40	6.63	8.60
Savings, national, gross, pesos	4.89	6.46	8.12
Investment − savings, pesos	0.51	0.17	0.48
Imports, current account excluding interest on debt, pesos	4.36	5.30	6.61
Exports, current account, pesos	3.97	5.18	6.65
Imports − exports = B^*, pesos	0.39	0.12	−0.04
= B^*, dollars	$41	$−3	$−32
Total balance of payments deficit = B Assumptions on debt service:‡			
$g = 0, i = 3\%, k = 15$ (a)		$27	$ 0
$g = 0, i = 5\%, k = 15$ (b)	$57	32	12
$g = 0, i = 3\%, k = 25$ (c)		27	0
$g = 10, i = 3\%, k = 15$ (d)		27	0
Capital flow other than public funds, net		0	0
Public debt outstanding, January 1			
(a)		$788	$872
(b)	$715§	790	914
(c)		788	872
(d)		788	872
Gross inflow of public funds			
(a)		$103	$63
(b)		109	78
(c)		97	49
(d)		88	28

† Period: 1954–1956 through 1959–1961.
‡ g = grace period, years
  i = interest on foreign debt
  k = amortization period, years
§ 1963.

4-5   KEY ESTIMATES D: COLOMBIA'S NATIONAL DEVELOPMENT PLAN SECTORAL RATES OF GROWTH

One of the purposes of the key estimates D, if not the principal one, is to explore the highly optimistic expectations of the National Development Plan of Colombia for the 1960s. Another purpose, irrespective of the expectations of Colombian planners, is to see what would be the implications of a very high rate of growth implying 3.2 per cent annual increase in per capita national product over the present decade.

The sectoral rates of growth used as a basis for key estimates D have been compiled from the Plan document (see Bibliography, no. 4). They yield an overall rate of growth of the economy of 6 per cent for the first half of the 1960s and 6.1 per cent for the second half of the decade. This rate falls between 5.7 per cent and 6.5 per cent, the "low" and "high" alternatives of the Plan. Because it was impossible to identify our own sectoral definitions except for agriculture with those used in the Plan (*Plan*, page 91) for the entire projection period, we used sectoral projections given in the Plan (page 141) for the first half of the 1960s, and we checked their consistency with the 10-year projections given in the Plan only for various aggregates based on our (eight) individual sectors of productive activity.

Key estimate D-1 is based on these sectoral rates of growth and on a set of other assumptions regarding the terms of trade, the rate of growth of coffee exports, and capital goods import substitution that can be termed least optimistic. The terms of trade are assumed to remain at their base-period level; and the output of domestic capital goods industries is expected to grow linearly, as it does in key estimates A-1, B-1, and C-1. Under these conditions the balance of payments deficit in 1970 is over $600 million assuming a 3 per cent rate of interest on public debt and almost $700 million assuming a 5 per cent rate of interest. The corresponding figures for gross borrowing with a zero grace period and a 15-year amortization period are $834 and $917 million respectively. The dominance of the foreign exchange gap over the savings-investment gap—already observed for the high rates of growth underlying key estimate B—again is found here.

The three remaining key estimates D (D-2 through D-4) are designed to show the principal avenues of possible improvement of the extremely high import-export gap obtained for key estimate D. The least unfavorable balance of payments situation is found for key estimate D-4, where, with a high (observed) rate of growth of the capital goods industries and an improvement in the terms of trade, the gap is reduced to a little over $300 million on the assumption of a 3 per cent rate of interest on public debt. The foreign exchange gap falls short of the savings-investment gap in this particular situation.

COLOMBIA: KEY ESTIMATES D

Basic assumptions specification: National Development Plan sectoral rates

Sectoral Rates of Growth	
Sector	*Rate*
1. Agriculture	0.043
2. Mining	0.074
3. Capital goods	0.083
4. Other manufactures	
5. Power	0.102
6. Construction	0.138
7. Transportation	0.062
8. All others	0.045
Overall	0.060

OTHER ASSUMPTIONS

1. No change in terms of trade between 1959–1961 and projection years.
2. Terms of trade T improve linearly to the 1958 level by 1970 ($T = +16.3\%$).
3. Rate of growth of coffee exports 0.028 (Source: B. Balassa).
5. Observed linear growth of capital goods industries:
   transportation equipment $V_3{}^{tr} = \bar{V}_3{}^{tr}(1 + 0.125t)$
   machinery $V_3{}^m = \bar{V}_3{}^m(1 + 0.156t)$
7. Exponential growth of capital goods industries:
   transportation equipment   0.10
   machinery   0.15
8. Observed exponential growth of capital goods industries:
   transportation equipment   0.12
   machinery   0.22

OTHER ASSUMPTIONS IN INDIVIDUAL KEY ESTIMATES

D-1: 1, 3, 5
D-2: 1, 3, 7
D-3: 2, 3, 7
D-4: 2, 3, 8

Assumptions Regarding Balance of Payments Deficit Financing			
Alternative	*Grace period g, years*	*Interest on foreign debt i, %*	*Amortization period k, years*
(a)	0	3	15
(b)	0	5	15
(c)	0	3	25
(d)	10	3	15

Colombia: Key Estimate D-1

(Valuation: constant 1960 prices and exchange rates; billion pesos and million dollars)

Basic assumptions specification: National Development Plan (1962) sectoral rates; no change in terms of trade; linear growth of capital goods production

Series description	Base period 1959–1961	1965	1970
Overall rate of growth of: GNP f.c.	.040†	.060	.061
Investment, gross, pesos	5.40	9.61	13.30
Savings, national, gross, pesos	4.89	6.86	10.10
Investment − savings, pesos	0.51	2.35	3.20
Imports, current account excluding interest on debt, pesos	4.36	6.73	9.39
Exports, current account, pesos	3.97	4.80	5.72
Imports − exports = B^*, pesos	0.39	1.93	3.67
= B^*, dollars	$41	$262	$511

Total balance of payments deficit = B
Assumptions on debt service:‡

			1965	1970
$g = 0, i = 3\%, k = 15$	(a)		$303	$615
$g = 0, i = 5\%, k = 15$	(b)	$57	316	682
$g = 0, i = 3\%, k = 25$	(c)		303	615
$g = 10, i = 3\%, k = 15$	(d)		303	682

		1965	1970
Capital flow other than public funds, net		0	0
Public debt outstanding, January 1			
	(a)	$1,163	$3,285
	(b)	1,169	3,446
	(c)	1,163	3,285
	(d)	1,163	3,285
Gross inflow of public funds			
	(a)	$404	$839
	(b)	418	917
	(c)	388	760
	(d)	364	643

† Period: 1954–1956 through 1959–1961.
‡ g = grace period, years
   i = interest on foreign debt
   k = amortization period, years
§ 1963.

Colombia: Key Estimate D-2

(Valuation: constant 1960 prices and exchange rates; billion pesos and million dollars)

Basic assumptions specification: National Development Plan (1962) sectoral rates; no change in terms of trade; exponential growth of capital goods production

Series description		Base period 1959–1961	1965	1970
Overall rate of growth of: GNP f.c.		.040†	.060	.061
Investment, gross, pesos		5.40	9.21	13.32
Savings, national, gross, pesos		4.89	6.86	10.14
Investment − savings, pesos		0.51	2.35	3.18
Imports, current account excluding interest on debt, pesos		4.36	4.80	5.72
Exports, current account, pesos		3.97	6.66	8.83
Imports − exports = B^*, pesos		0.39	1.86	3.11
= B^*, dollars		$41	$252	$430
Total balance of payments deficit = B Assumptions on debt service:‡				
$g = 0, i = 3\%, k = 15$	(a)		$293	$528
$g = 0, i = 5\%, k = 15$	(b)	$57	305	590
$g = 0, i = 3\%, k = 25$	(c)		293	528
$g = 10, i = 3\%, k = 15$	(d)		293	528
Capital flow other than public funds, net			0	0
Public debt outstanding, January 1				
	(a)		$1,149	$3,076
	(b)	$715§	1,155	3,229
	(c)		1,149	3,076
	(d)		1,149	3,076
Gross inflow of public funds				
	(a)		$393	$738
	(b)		406	810
	(c)		378	665
	(d)		354	556

† Period: 1954–1956 through 1959–1961.
‡ g = grace period, years
  i = interest on foreign debt
  k = amortization period, years
§ 1963.

Colombia: Key Estimate D-3

(Valuation: constant 1960 prices and exchange rates; billion pesos and million dollars)

Basic assumptions specification: National Development Plan (1962) sectoral rates, return in terms of trade to 1958 level; exponential growth of capital goods production

Series description		Base period 1959–1961	1965	1970
Overall rate of growth of: GNP f.c.		.040†	.060	.061
Investment, gross, pesos		5.40	9.21	13.32
Savings, national, gross, pesos		4.89	7.29	10.68
Investment − savings, pesos		0.51	1.92	2.64
Imports, current account excluding interest on debt, pesos		4.36	6.66	8.83
Exports, current account, pesos		3.97	5.09	6.42
Imports − exports = B^*, pesos		0.39	1.57	2.41
= B^*, dollars		$41	$208	$325
Total balance of payments deficit = B Assumptions on debt service:‡				
$g = 0, i = 3\%, k = 15$	(a)		$247	$410
$g = 0, i = 5\%, k = 15$	(b)	$57	256	462
$g = 0, i = 3\%, k = 25$	(c)		247	410
$g = 10, i = 3\%, k = 15$	(d)		247	410
Capital flow other than public funds, net			0	0
Public debt outstanding, January 1				
	(a)		$1,087	$2,646
	(b)	$715§	1,092	2,777
	(c)		1,087	2,646
	(d)		1,087	2,646
Gross inflow of public funds				
	(a)		$343	$591
	(b)		353	652
	(c)		329	530
	(d)		308	438

† Period: 1954–1956 through 1959–1961.
‡ g = grace period, years
i = interest on foreign debt
k = amortization period, years
§ 1963.

Colombia: Key Estimate D-4

(Valuation: constant 1960 prices and exchange rates; billion pesos and million dollars)

Basic assumptions specification: National Development Plan (1962) sectoral rates; no change in terms of trade; high observed exponential rates of growth of capital goods production

Series description	Base period 1959–1961	1965	1970
Overall rate of growth of: GNP f.c.	.040†	.060	.061
Investment, gross, pesos	5.40	9.21	13.32
Savings, national, gross, pesos	4.89	6.86	10.14
Investment − savings, pesos	0.51	2.35	3.18
Imports, current account excluding interest on debt, pesos	4.36	6.37	7.54
Exports, current account, pesos	3.97	4.80	5.72
Imports − exports = B^*, pesos	0.39	1.57	1.82
= B^*, dollars	$41	$210	$242

Total balance of payments deficit = B
Assumptions on debt service:‡

		Base period 1959–1961	1965	1970
$g = 0, i = 3\%, k = 15$	(a)		$249	$322
$g = 0, i = 5\%, k = 15$	(b)	$57	258	371
$g = 0, i = 3\%, k = 25$	(c)		249	322
$g = 10, i = 3\%, k = 15$	(d)		249	322
Capital flow other than public funds, net			0	0

Public debt outstanding, January 1

		Base period 1959–1961	1965	1970
	(a)		$1,088	$2,480
	(b)	$715§	1,093	2,607
	(c)		1,088	2,480
	(d)		1,088	2,480

Gross inflow of public funds

		Base period 1959–1961	1965	1970
	(a)		$345	$492
	(b)		355	550
	(c)		331	435
	(d)		310	350

† Period: 1954–1956 through 1959–1961.
‡ g = grace period, years
  i = interest on foreign debt
  k = amortization period, years
§ 1963.

4-6 COMPARISON OF THE KEY ESTIMATES WITH OTHER PROJECTIONS FOR COLOMBIA

There is one other subject that ought to be taken up in this part of the study.   The key estimates A presented here are based on sectoral rates of growth taken from the report by the Committee of Nine.   The same source also gives estimates of the balance of payments for Colombia in 1965.   Moreover, the International Bank for Reconstruction and Development has produced balance of payments estimates for 1965 and 1970. Our key estimates D, on the other hand, are designed to test the consistency of the National Development Plan of Colombia.   Consequently, these estimates ought to be compared with the projections of balance of payments contained in the National Plan document.

We have to limit ourselves here to the comparison of final results. None of the sources just mentioned contains satisfactory, if any, exposition of the methods by which the estimates of future gaps were obtained; consequently, it is impossible to confront these projections with our own work in an analytical fashion.

In Table 4-1 we compare the foreign exchange gap—i.e., the balance of payments on current account—of our key estimate A-1 with the Committee of Nine projections and the IBRD projections respectively.

Table 4-1. Comparison of Balance of Payments Projections

(In millions of U.S. dollars)

Description	1959–1961 (*actual*)	1965	1970
Exports of goods and services:			
Our alternative A-1	$592	$ 725	$ 878
Committee of Nine		699	
IBRD		600	660
Imports of goods (f.o.b.) and services:			
Our alternative A-1 †	649	858	1,120
Committee of Nine		961	
IBRD		725	890–910
Balance of payments on current account:			
Our alternative A-1 †	−57	−133	−242
Committee of Nine		−262	
IBRD		−125	−230–250

† Assuming 3 per cent rate of interest paid on new debt.

With respect to deficit financing, our A-1 estimate is based on a "low" assumption of interest on new public debt, namely, 3 per cent. This rate of interest is about 0.8 per cent below that actually observed in the recent past.

The first thing that will be noticed is a remarkable similarity between the IBRD balance of payments estimates and our own for 1965 and 1970. However, considering the individual export and import figures entering these balance of payments estimates, the picture becomes a good deal less satisfactory. The IBRD export and import estimates are both considerably below ours. Let it only be noted that the IBRD export estimate for 1965 of $600 million was about realized in 1962, even though this was a year of "bottom" terms of trade for Colombia. On the import side it is impossible to explain the wide difference without knowing the assumptions used for the IBRD projection. But again a pragmatic argument can be made: namely, the actual imports of goods and services in 1962 came to within 1 per cent of the 1965 IBRD projection.

The estimates produced for 1965 by the Committee of Nine, on the other hand, appear too pessimistic, and inconsistent with the sectoral rates of growth assumed by the Committee. Actually, there is a strong presumption that with a foreign exchange gap of $262 million in 1965 and correspondingly growing deficits between 1960 and 1965, the Colombian economy could have attained a good deal higher rate of growth in the first half of the 1960s than the 4.9 per cent postulated by the Committee. This conclusion becomes quite plausible if we consider, say, our key estimate B-1.

Actually if the improvement in the terms of trade (prices of coffee) observed in late 1963 and early 1964 either continues or at least endures, even our own and the IBRD gap estimates can be deemed rather pessimistic for the situation where the Colombian economy would grow at only 5 per cent. With that rate of growth a better estimate of the balance of payments situation in 1965 and 1970 would then be our key estimate A-2.

The second comparison we want to make is that between our estimates based on the sectoral rates as implied in the Colombia National Plan and the balance of payments projections of the National Plan. The relevant data are shown in Table 4-2. It will be recalled that the overall rates of growth for the 1960s expected by the Plan are very high: 5.6 and 6.5 per cent for the low and high alternatives respectively (for further discussion of the assumption see section 4-5). And consequently, the foreign exchange gaps corresponding to these rates could be expected prima facie to be well above the gaps just discussed, corresponding to a considerably lower overall growth rate.

However, this expectation is not borne out at all by the projections con-

Table 4-2. Comparison of Balance of Payments Projections

(In millions of current U.S. dollars)

Description	1959–1961 (actual)	1965	1970
Exports of goods and services:			
Our alternative D-2†	$ 592	$ 715	$ 852
National Development Plan (hyp. A)‡		822	1,073
National Development Plan (hyp. B)‡		822	1,073
Imports of goods and services:			
Our alternative D-2	649	1,008	1,380
National Development Plan (hyp. A)		896	1,028
National Development Plan (hyp. B)		936	1,105
Balance of payments on current account:			
Our alternative D-2	−57	−293	−528
National Development Plan (hyp. A)		−74	45
National Development Plan (hyp. B)		−114	−32

† Based on the sectoral rates of growth of the National Development Plan with no change in the terms of trade and exponential growth of the capital goods industry; to obtain our B from B^* we assumed a 3 per cent rate of interest on new debt.

‡ Hypotheses A and B assume 5.6 and 6.5 per cent aggregate rates of growth of gross domestic product respectively.   The aggregate rate implied in our D-2 is about 6.1 per cent.   The balance of payments figures for the National Development Plan for 1965 and 1970 are linear interpolations of projections for 1962–1964, 1965–1967, and 1968–1970.

tained in the Plan.   Assuming no change in the terms of trade and using sectoral rates of growth adding up to an overall rate just about halfway between the rates of hypotheses A and B, we obtain a foreign exchange gap of over $500 million for 1970.   The gap projected by the Plan, on the other hand, is negligible on the less favorable hypothesis and turns into a balance of payments surplus on the more favorable assumption. The differences are less striking for 1965.

It will be noted that the key estimate D-2 we are using here is based on relatively high assumed rates of growth of the capital goods industries, and hence on a good deal of import substitution.   Also, we have used a very favorable assumption regarding the rate of interest on newly con- tracted debt in the 1960s, namely, a rate of 3 per cent.   The one factor that could substantially improve the picture from that indicated by our key estimate would be an improvement in coffee prices.   However, these prices would have to increase by about 100 per cent, compared with the base period, to obtain results comparable with the Plan projections for 1970.

Chapter **5** THE SENSITIVITY ANALYSIS

5-1 THE PURPOSE AND METHOD OF SENSITIVITY ANALYSIS

Although we have made a serious effort to design as adequate an estimation structure as possible, given data availability and our research
resources, we do not pretend that the structure we are using in predicting
future aid requirements is flawless.   Errors of observation are one possible source of imperfection.   Even in the absence of such errors it may
well be that structural parameters derived from past performance will
change in the future.   Moreover, the sectoral rates of growth—the
principal predetermined variables—cannot be known exactly for the
future 10 or 15 years, and consequently, none of our key projections
(see Chapter 4) may reflect the true state of future events.

These and other possible sources of error lead us to perform what we
call the "sensitivity analysis" of our estimates.   In essence, the purpose
of this analysis is to show in a simple way how the various estimates of
future gaps depend on different elements of the estimation structure.
To give an example, suppose that an estimate of the balance of payments
(excluding interest on public debt) B^* is obtained for 1970; one possible
answer sought through the sensitivity analysis then is: By how much and
in what direction will B^* change if the capital-output coefficient for indus-

trial production in Colombia is 10 per cent different from that actually used in the estimation procedure—or, alternatively, if the rate of growth of the agricultural sector changes by 1 per cent point?

If at a later stage better information on any parameter used in our procedure can be obtained, the estimates presented here can easily be adjusted. Alternatively, range estimates rather than point estimates of future aid requirements can be calculated using the sensitivity analysis. For example, we may ask what the range is of possible foreign exchange gaps corresponding to an expected (or likely) range (say 10 per cent) of the terms of trade in 1970.

It ought to be noted that the sensitivity analysis showing the various relations between parameters on the one hand and the foreign resource requirements on the other is highly relevant for the present study. At a later stage, in Part 3, we examine the adjustment mechanism of the two gaps estimated in relation to economic policies, actual level of aid, and more or less autonomous economic forces. Such an analysis could not be carried out satisfactorily if we did not have at least approximate knowledge of the various relations between the gaps and the underlying parameters.

There are several possible ways of computing sensitivity indices. The particular index we have decided to use is the "transformation elasticity," defined as the per cent change in a given gap estimate corresponding to a 1 per cent change in a structural parameter (such as sectoral rate of growth r, foreign demand parameter f, a structural coefficient k, or policy parameter p). We prefer the elasticity concept to others because of its invariance with respect to changes in units of measurement.

Letting g represent one of the two gaps (IS and B^*), and z_i one of the four groups of parameters ($r, f, k,$ and p), the elasticity of transformation e_i corresponding to parameter z_i is formally defined as

$$e_i = \frac{\partial g/\partial z_i}{g/z_i} \tag{5-1}$$

The elasticities of transformation can easily be calculated from the explicit forms of the two gaps IS and B^*, derived from relations for the four basic aggregates presented in section 3-7 for any of the key estimates presented in Chapter 4. Because the mathematical formulation of the gaps does not involve any complicated functions, the partial derivatives in the numerator of relation (5-1) can be obtained in most cases without difficulty. Only one remark is in order in this context: most of the functions entering the procedure contain terms such as $(1 + r_{ijk})^t \bar{V}_{ijk}$ or this term (in the acceleration relations) multiplied by r_{ijk}. For the purpose of partial differentiation it must be recalled that

$$(1 + r_{ijk})^t \bar{V}_{ijk} = \sum_{p=i,j,k} (1 + r_p)^t \bar{V}_p \tag{5-2}$$

and that

$$r_{ijk}(1 + r_{ijk})^t \bar{V}_{ijk} = \sum_{p=i,j,k} r_p(1 + r_p)^t \bar{V}_p \qquad (5\text{-}3)$$

If then a partial derivative with respect to a single rate of growth is sought, only one term in the summation on the right has to be differentiated, all other partial derivatives being zero. It will also be recalled that relations (5-2) and (5-3) hold for any number of sectors, including the case of $ijk = 1, 2, \ldots, 8$, that is, including the case where total gross domestic product is the predetermined variable.

One important word of caution must be said regarding use of the transformation elasticities. Let us use an example. Suppose that the transformation elasticity relating the foreign exchange gap B^* and a given capital-output coefficient K is 0.2. In other words, a 1 per cent change in K produces a $\frac{1}{5}$ of 1 per cent positive change in B^*. If then it is believed that the true value of the capital-output coefficient is 10 per cent higher than what was assumed in our estimation procedure, the conclusions would be that B^* as calculated in the key estimates (see Chapter 4) must be corrected upward by 2 per cent. This figure is very close to the true change in B^* that would be obtained if a completely new calculation were performed using the new capital coefficient, but generally *not exactly* the true change (the latter may be, for example, 1.95 per cent). Thus, results of calculations based on the transformation elasticities can give only approximations. These approximations will be the more satisfactory, the smaller the change in the parameter (such as K in our example). For large changes in parameters—such as, for example, doubling of K—the approximations obtained will not be very accurate, and consequently, if such cases were to arise, the whole gap ought to be recalculated using the new evidence and using the estimation procedure (for the latter, see Chapter 3).

There is one important difference between the sectoral rates r and the other parameters f, k, and p. Whereas changes in the former affect the overall rate of growth of the economy, changes in the latter do not (in the context of our procedure). Consequently, it will be convenient to present the transformation elasticities for sectoral rates together with another indicator, namely, the per cent effect of a 1 per cent change in sectoral rate r_i on the expected value of gross domestic product, that is, on V.

Although the gap transformation elasticities are the principal output of this part of the study, we tabulate in the subsequent sections another set of useful results, namely, the transformation elasticities for savings, investment, imports, and exports. These elasticities, e_s, e_i, e_m, and e_e respectively, show the per cent change of each of the four aggregates corresponding to a 1 per cent change in a given parameter. The gap transformation elasticities are weighted differences of the corresponding elasticities e. For example, the investment-savings gap transformation elasticity e_{is} is given by

$$e_{is} = \frac{Ie_i - Se_s}{I - S} \tag{5-4}$$

where I and S are investment and savings in the projection year (e.g., 1970).

5-2 SENSITIVITY ANALYSIS OF KEY ESTIMATE A-1: SECTORAL RATES OF GROWTH

The sensitivity analysis explained in the preceding section is applied to only one of the 13 key estimates, namely, key estimate A-1, based on sectoral rates of growth assumed by the Committee of Nine of the Alliance for Progress. Exact specifications of this key estimate are given in section 4-2. We have limited the sensitivity analysis to only one case for two reasons: (1) For a single case the necessary computational effort is already quite considerable; and (2) even more important, for the range of outcomes that can be reasonably expected, the transformation elasticities derived for a single key estimate can be expected to yield satisfactory approximations to the impact of changing parameters. Actually, it was this second consideration that led us to the selection of the median estimate A-1.

Also it should be recalled from section 4-2 that the key estimate A-1 is the only one carried to year 1975. This was done primarily to create a basis for a sensitivity analysis. The key estimate A-1 for 1975 unavoidably is subject to a considerable margin of possible error. Within the 15 years separating the base period from 1975 many unpredictable changes can take place. Consequently, it is more important to have for 1975 a tool of evaluating the changes in economic conditions than to have a point estimate based on rigidly set assumptions.

The sensitivity analysis is carried out only for 1970 and 1975. We omit the first projection year: results obtained in Chapter 4 are considered sufficient for that year.

In this section we present the results of the sensitivity analysis of key estimate A-1 with respect to sectoral rates of growth. The transformation elasticities of investment, savings, imports, and exports are given in Table 5-1, and the corresponding transformation elasticities for the balance of payments and savings-investment gaps are presented in Table 5-2. Because the sectoral rates of growth—unlike other parameters—affect not only the size of the gaps but also the overall rate of

Table 5-1. Colombia: Transformation Elasticities of Investment, Savings, Imports, and Exports with Respect to (A) Sectoral Rates of Growth, 1970 and 1975

Rate of growth of	Investment		Savings		Imports		Exports	
	1970	1975	1970	1975	1970	1975	1970	1975
1. Agriculture	.031	.041	.049	.072	.034	.045	−.028	−.040
2. Mining	.122	.149	.151	.200	.094	.115	−.007	−.012
3. Capital goods manufacturing	.085	.070	.084	.090	−.114	−.148	−.004	−.005
4. Noncapital goods manufacturing	.476	.566	.596	.779	.409	.507	−.028	−.046
5. Construction	.227	.324	.204	.297	.187	.235	−.012	−.021
6. Electricity, gas, and water	.050	.204	.097	.176	.095	.160	−.005	−.011
7. Transportation and communications	.252	.287	.249	.296	.260	.300	−.009	−.015
8. All others	.040	.055	.063	.095	.044	.060	−.036	−.054

growth of the economy, we have calculated indicators of the impact of sectoral rates on total domestic product. These indicators show the per cent change in gross domestic product in the projection year resulting from a 1 per cent change in the rate of growth of a given sector (see Table 5-3).

The formulas used in computing the transformation elasticities are given in Appendix B. Observe that the sensitivity analysis for any key estimate (other than A-1 examined here) can be based on these formulas since the basic functions are the same.

Let us now turn to the most important of the three tables, namely, Table 5-2, where the transformation elasticities are tabulated for the two gaps. It will be recalled that the foreign exchange gap B^* represents the current balance of payments excluding interest on debt; consequently, the total balance of payments B will be larger than B^*, the difference between the two depending primarily on the rate of interest on foreign debt (to evaluate this difference consult the key estimates in Chapter 4). However, the elasticities of transformation for B^* may be either greater or smaller than those that would be obtained for B. This is so because introducing the interest on debt into the balance of payments would increase both B and the change in B resulting from a given change in a sectoral rate of growth.

Table 5-2. Colombia: Elasticities of Transformation: Gap Sensitivity Analysis.
Key Estimate A-1

(Per cent change in gap indicated on top of table per 1 per cent change in
parameter listed on the left)

Year	1970		1975	
Gap type	*B**	*IS*	*B**	*IS*
Size, in billion pesos, 1960	1.41	2.12	2.56	3.04
Size, as proportion of V	.035	.052	.049	.058
Parameters				
A. Sectoral rates of growth				
Sector:				
1. Agriculture	.29	−.04	.29	−.07
2. Mining	.51	.01	.48	−.04
3. Capital goods manufacturing	−.56	.09	−.56	−.00
4. Noncapital goods manufacturing	2.23	.01	2.09	−.20
5. Construction	1.02	.31	.97	.42
6. Electricity, gas, and water	.51	−.13	.65	.31
7. Transportation and communication	1.38	.26	1.20	.25
8. All others	.38	−.05	.38	−.09

The first thing that will be observed is that as a general rule the transformation elasticities for the foreign exchange gap are larger than those for the savings-investment gap. For example, a 10 per cent increase in the rate of growth of the construction industry over the 1960s would increase $B*$ by about 10 per cent, while the savings-investment gap would go up by only about 3 per cent. This general result is a natural consequence of the rigidity of export earnings typical for the developing countries and the comparative responsiveness of savings to changes in the overall rate of growth of the economy. This responsiveness is even better illustrated by the manufacturing industry excluding capital goods; an increase in the rate of growth of this sector will have just about no effect on the savings-investment gap in 1970 and will reduce that gap by 1975, while enlarging the balance of payments gap considerably in both years.

The comparative improvement (reduction) of the transformation elasticities for the savings-investment gap between 1970 and 1975 is another general pattern revealed by Table 5-2. It clearly stems from the fact that changes in rates of growth are translated much more promptly into investment requirement than into increased savings; indeed, savings become large from a higher growth rate only after a number of years when the current aggregate upon which savings depend becomes large itself. It is the same phenomenon that explains the comparative decline in importance of the savings-investment gap with respect to the foreign exchange gap observed for the key estimates in Chapter 4.

To the significance of the data recorded in Table 5-3 we shall return in section 5-4 in greater detail. At this point let us only say that they complement the transformation elasticity tabulations in the sense that they make it possible to evaluate the impact of sectoral rates of growth on the overall level of economic progress. Information on that impact is not contained in the transformation elasticities themselves.

Table 5-3. Colombia: Transformation Elasticities of Gross Domestic Product V with Respect to Sectoral Rates of Growth r_i, $\left(\dfrac{\partial V}{\partial r_i}\dfrac{r_i}{V}\right)$

Rate of growth of	1970	1975
1. Agriculture	.106	.147
2. Mining	.027	.043
3. Capital goods manufacturing	.014	.018
4. Noncapital goods manufacturing	.106	.167
5. Construction	.044	.078
6. Electricity, gas, and water	.020	.041
7. Transportation and communications	.035	.054
8. All others	.136	.197

5-3 SENSITIVITY ANALYSIS OF KEY ESTIMATE A-1: STRUCTURAL PARAMETERS

In this section we examine the relation between structural parameters appearing in our estimation procedure and the magnitudes of investment, savings, imports, exports, the foreign exchange gap B^*, and the savings-investment gap IS. As explained in section 5-1 the indicator of these relationships is the transformation elasticity. The method of computing the transformation elasticities of the structural parameters is further explained in Appendix B.

The transformation elasticities are recorded here in two tables. The first, Table 5-4, contains the transformation elasticities of investment, savings, imports, and exports. Note that only one elasticity appears here for exports because most of the parameters in the export function

Table 5-4. Colombia: Transformation Elasticities of Investment, Savings, Imports, and
Exports with Respect to (B) Structural Parameters

Parameter	1970	1975
Investment:		
Average investment rate in buildings	.21	.20
Incremental capital-output ratio for construction	.30	.31
Incremental capital-output ratio for machinery	.29	.31
Incremental capital-output ratio for transportation equipment	.11	.11
Average investment rate in inventories	.08	.08
Savings:		
Relation between depreciation and gross domestic fixed investment	.45	.45
Average corporate profit rate on value-added	.29	.30
Relation between rates of growth of income and property taxes and gross domestic product	.12	.17
Average rate of government spending on current account	− .40	− .38
Relation between terms of trade, and saving, by household and indirect government taxes as a proportion of gross domestic product	.39	.37
Imports:		
Average import rate of raw materials	.07	.07
Average import rate of fuels	.03	.03
Average import rate of base metals	.08	.08
Average import rate of machinery	.41	.43
Average output value-added relationship for machinery	− .12	− .16
Average import rate of transportation equipment	.16	.15
Average output value-added relationship for transportation equipment	− .08	− .07
Average import rate for other visible imports	.28	.28
Average relationship between the rates of growth of produced services and gross domestic product	.02	.02
Exports:		
Domestic income elasticity of demand for petroleum and petroleum products	− .10	− .14

are classified as "foreign condition parameters" and are examined separately in the following section.   In the other table, Table 5-5, we tabulate
the transformation elasticities for the two gaps.   Contrary to the elasticities discussed in the preceding section, each individual parameter
generally affects only one of the two gaps, because each parameter appears
only in one of the four underlying aggregates.   The description of the
parameters appearing in the table often does not fully explain the meaning of the parameter.   For the exact meaning the reader is advised to
turn to Chapter 3, and to section 3-7 in particular.   As in the preceding
section, the tables containing the gap transformation elasticities show the

Table 5-5. Colombia: Elasticities of Transformation: Gap Sensitivity Analysis.
Key Estimate A-1

(Per cent change in gap indicated on top of table per 1 per cent change in
parameter listed on the left)

Year	1970		1975	
Gap type	B*	IS	B*	IS
Size, in billion pesos, 1960	1.41	2.12	2.56	3.04
Size, as proportion of V	.035	.052	.049	.058

Parameters

B. Structural parameters
  Investment:

	B*	IS	B*	IS
Average investment rate in buildings	0	1.01	0	.91
Incremental capital-output ratio for construction	0	1.44	0	1.41
Incremental capital-output ratio for machinery	2.12	1.41	1.68	1.41
Incremental capital-output ratio for transportation equipment	.83	.55	.60	.50
Average investment rate in inventories	0	.40	0	.36

  Savings:

Relation between depreciation and gross domestic fixed investment	0	−1.71	0	−1.63
Average corporate profit rates on value-added	0	−1.12	0	−1.06
Relation between rates of growth of income and property taxes and gross domestic product	0	−.45	0	−.62
Average rate of government spending on current account	0	1.51	0	1.36
Relation between terms of trade and saving by house-				

Table 5-5. Colombia: Elasticities of Transformation: Gap Sensitivity Analysis.
Key Estimate A-1 (Continued)

Year	1970		1975	
Gap type	B*	IS	B*	IS
Size, in billion pesos, 1960	1.41	2.12	2.56	3.04
Size, as proportion of V	.035	.052	.049	.058
holds and indirect government taxes as a proportion of gross domestic product	0	−1.50	0	−1.35
Imports:				
Average import rate of raw materials	.34	0	.27	0
Average import rate of fuels	.13	0	.10	0
Average import rate of base metals	.40	0	.31	0
Incremental capital-output ratio for machinery (in sectors 2 to 6)	2.12	1.41	1.68	1.41
Average output value-added relationship for machinery	−.65	0	−.63	0
Incremental capital-output ratio for transportation equipment	.83	.55	.60	.50
Average output value-added relationship for transportation equipment	−.44	0	−.26	0
Average import rate for other visible imports	1.48	0	1.06	0
Average relationship between rates of growth of imports of produced services and gross domestic product	.10	0	.09	0
Exports:				
Domestic income elasticity of demand for petroleum and petroleum products	.41	0	41	0

magnitudes of the gaps estimated for 1970 and 1975. These numbers make it possible for us to evaluate directly from the information in the table the effect—either in billions of pesos or as a share of domestic product—of a given change in a parameter on the size of the gaps.

To give an illustration, observe that the balance of payments transformation elasticity for the capital-output coefficient for machinery (in sectors 2, 3, 4, 5, and 6) in 1970 is 2.12 (which happens to be the highest elasticity observed). Consequently, a 10 per cent increase in the capital-output ratio for machinery would increase the foreign exchange gap by about 21 per cent, that is, by about 0.15 billion pesos (about $22 million). Note that the capital-output coefficient used is 3.33; consequently, the 10 per cent increase would lead to a coefficient of 3.66.[1]

Another transformation elasticity that ought to be discussed briefly is that for the average propensity to import "other imports." The elasticity is 1.48 for 1970 and 1.06 for 1975. We have already noted in Chapter 3 that this average propensity to import, of all the import parameters, is the one most readily amenable to policy controls. For one thing, the "other imports" aggregate includes imports of finished consumer goods; such imports can be reduced—of course, at the cost of certain hardships for the consumer—without affecting the gross domestic product or its growth and, consequently, without having any effect on the rate of growth of the economy (exogenous in our structure). Another fact to be considered is that in the Colombian National Plan a reduction of such "nonessential" imports is envisaged.[2]

The transformation elasticity for "other imports" is thus an extremely useful tool in evaluating the possibilities of reducing the foreign exchange gap in the future. According to the Colombia National Plan document, all consumer goods imports (durable and nondurable) in the base period were about 8 per cent of total imports. The figure for our aggregate of "other imports" is about 30 per cent. Consequently, the transformation elasticity for consumer goods imports for 1970 is 0.395, and for 1975, 0.283.[3] Thus, for example, if the imports of consumer goods were cut by

[1] It is apparent from this calculation that efficiency of capital, and its full utilization, is an important factor affecting the foreign exchange (and/or savings) requirements. If domestic or foreign exchange costs were involved in reducing the capital-output coefficient—say, through education, foreign technical assistance, or other means—then the transformation elasticities computed here could be used in evaluating the desirability of such capital-saving measures. A parallel argument for the sectoral rate transformation elasticities is further explored in section 5-5.

[2] Government of Colombia, Consejo Nacional de Politica Economica y Planeacion, *Plan General de Desarrollo Economico y Social, Parte I-General*, Cali, Colombia: Banco de la Republica, 1962, p. 319.

[3] The implicit assumption here is that over the projection period imports of consumer goods and the rest of the "other imports" remained in a constant proportion to each other. For a further elaboration on this point see Appendix B.

25 per cent in 1970 compared with what they would have been on the assumptions underlying our import function, the foreign exchange gap in 1970 would have been reduced by about 10 per cent, that is, 0.14 billion pesos.

5-4 SENSITIVITY ANALYSIS OF KEY ESTIMATE A-1: FOREIGN CONDITIONS

Our key estimates reflect alternative assumptions regarding future prices and export volumes of coffee.   The paramount importance of coffee in Colombia's exports and the comparative uncertainty about the future of the world coffee market warrant the inclusion of these assumptions into the key estimates.   However, there are other parameters in the export function whose impact on the gap estimates must also be ascertained.   Moreover, the terms of trade not only affect export earning, but also, as explained in Chapter 3, relate to the rate of savings.   Both

Table 5-6. Colombia: Transformation Elasticities of Imports, Exports, and Savings with Respect to (C) Foreign Conditions

Parameter	1970	1975
Imports:		
Average relation between remittance and net worth of foreign enterprises	.05	.05
Rate of growth of net worth of foreign enterprises	.02	.03
Exports:		
World market price of coffee	.50	.47
External terms of trade	.73†	.69†
Rate of growth of coffee exports	.14	.19
World market price of petroleum	.10	.08
Rate of growth of other visible exports	.14	.23
Rate of growth of exports of services	.14	.23
Savings:		
External terms of trade	.39	.37
World market price of coffee	.27†	.26†

† We assume here that the external terms of trade increase through a rise in the world market price of coffee (petroleum, other export and import prices remaining unchanged).   Therefore, an increase in the terms of trade by 16.3 per cent between 1960 and 1970 corresponds to a 23.7 per cent increase in world coffee prices; thus the multiplier between the elasticities of both exports and savings with respect to the two related parameters (world market price of coffee and external terms of trade) is 23.7:16.3 or 1.454.

the terms of trade and the other export parameters are primarily a function of foreign economic conditions.

The transformation elasticities for the foreign condition parameters are presented here in two tables. The first (Table 5-6) shows the elasticities of exports, imports, and savings; the second (Table 5-7) shows the elasticities of the two gaps.

Table 5-7. Colombia: Elasticities of Transformation: Gap Sensitivity Analysis. Key Estimate A-1

(Per cent change in gap indicated on top of table per 1 per cent change in parameter listed on the left)

Year	1970		1975	
Gap type	B*	IS	B*	IS
Size, in billion pesos, 1960	1.41	2.12	2.56	3.04
Size, as proportion of V	.035	.052	.049	.058
Parameters				
C. Foreign conditions				
Imports:				
Average relation between remittance and net worth of foreign enterprises	.26	0	.18	0
Rate of growth of net worth of foreign enterprises	.12	.13	.13	0
Exports:				
World market price of coffee	−2.09	0	−1.35	0
External terms of trade	−3.04	0	−1.97	0
Rate of growth of coffee exports	−.57	0	−.54	0
World market price of petroleum	−.40	0	−.22	0
Rate of growth of other visible exports	−.57	0	−.67	0
Rate of growth of exports of services	−.57	0	−.66	0
Savings:				
External terms of trade	0	−1.50	0	−1.35
World market price of coffee	0	−1.03	0	−.99

Only a few indices in Table 5-7 deserve special attention.   By far the most important transformation elasticity is that for the terms of trade. In 1970, for example, a 1 per cent improvement in the terms of trade would produce a 3 per cent reduction in the foreign exchange gap and a 1.5 per cent reduction in the savings-investment gap, that is, reductions of about 40 and 30 million pesos respectively.   Similar effects, but reduced roughly in proportion of coffee exports to total exports, are found for the export price of coffee.

5-5   THE SENSITIVITY ANALYSIS AND EFFICIENT SCARCE RESOURCE ALLOCATION

In section 5-2 we presented the gap transformation elasticities (Table 5-2) together with total national income elasticities (Table 5-3).   Taking the ratio between the latter magnitude and the IS and B^* gaps for the ith sector, we get the two numbers

$$n_1{}^i = \left(\frac{\partial V/\partial (IS)}{V/IS}\right)_i \tag{5-5}$$

and

$$n_2{}^i = \left(\frac{\partial V/\partial B^*}{V/B^*}\right)_i \tag{5-6}$$

respectively.

The exact meaning of the first number [relation (5-5)] is the per cent increase in the national product in the projection year corresponding to a 1 per cent increase in the savings-investment gap, the increased resources (corresponding to the increased gap) being used in augmenting the rate of growth of sector i.   An analogous definition obtains for $n_2{}^i$, with B^* substituted for the savings-investment gap.

The comparison of the n's for two sectors (i and j) then yields an indicator of comparative productivity, or efficiency, of additional foreign resources for the economy.   To give an example, the index for the building and construction sector $n_2{}^5$ equals 0.043 for Colombia in 1970, and the index for the manufacturing other than capital goods sector $n_2{}^4$ is equal to 0.048.   In words, an increase in foreign resources spreading over the projection period 1960–1970 and leading (after all repercussions are taken into account) to an increase in foreign resource requirements of 1 per cent by 1970 would lead to an increase of gross domestic product in that year equal to 0.048 per cent if the additional foreign resources were used to boost the rate of growth of sector 4 and to an increase of 0.043 per cent if the same resources were used in increasing the rate of growth of sector 5.[4]

It is clear that this criterion is not the only one that a less developed country should or could use in allocating marginal resources. Other considerations, such as demand, price variation (note that our entire procedure is based, with the exception of external terms of trade, on constant price valuation), and a number of others, are also relevant. However, the comparison of the different n-indices can be considered a valuable tool of an optimizing planning procedure.

An additional problem arises concerning which of the two index comparisons—that based on the savings-investment gap or that based on the foreign exchange gap—should be used. We shall return to this problem in greater detail and in another context in Part 3. At this point a provisional answer can be provided: The index based on the dominant, that is, the larger of the two gaps, should be selected for comparison—of course, on the assumption that the gap itself will be financed.

If one or both gaps cannot be financed, then the criterion suggested here can in turn serve as guidance for an orderly reduction of plan targets consistent with economic optimum. For example, were the foreign exchange gap dominant in Colombia in 1970 and were there no hope that resources implied by that gap (see our key estimate A-1) would be obtainable in that year, it would be preferable—using the criteria here considered—to reduce the rate of growth of the construction industry rather than that of manufacturing of noncapital goods.

But the analysis suggested here need not be limited to the evaluation of effects of foreign resources. Suppose that it is the savings-investment gap that is dominant. In that case, additional domestic investment resources are as valuable as foreign resources to the developing economy, and the question can be asked how to allocate optimally additional domestic savings obtained, say, from increased taxation.

Although conceptually correct, the criteria discussed thus far *in abstracto* are only of limited value when we use our projection structure derived for Colombia. This is so because of the crudeness of the estimation procedure adopted here. Lack of adequate sectoral data on investment, imports, savings, and exports made it impossible to relate each of the four central aggregates to estimates of value-added for individual sectors. In most cases we were forced to use relations involving several sectors combined as explanatory variables; moreover, these aggregations had to include different sectors for different functions. Consequently,

[4] As an illustration, observe that these percentages would imply a 17 million-peso increase in national product for $n_2{}^5$ and a 19 million-peso increase for $n_2{}^4$ resulting from an increase of 14 million pesos (1 per cent) in the foreign exchange gap in 1970.

the indices n^i based on our sensitivity analysis cannot be very good estimates of the true values of the n's. It can only be said that they will be the better, the closer the *average* structural parameters in our procedure, relating value-added in several sectors to a dependent variable, are to the individual (true) parameters that would have been obtained if sectors had not to be aggregated. But it should be clear that no close similarity between the average and individual parameters can be expected in the real world. For example, the average capital-output coefficient that we have derived for the combination of sectors 2 to 6 certainly cannot be expected to equal each and every individual sectoral capital-output coefficient.

Nevertheless, these considerations should not detract from the fact that the application of the sensitivity analysis discussed here can be a very useful and operational tool of development planning. This is especially so in view of the impossibility of constructing any more refined planning procedures, involving a complete dynamic general equilibrium model.

The indices of sectoral efficiency of resource allocation n_1^i and n_2^i derived for 1970 from data in section 5-2 are presented below.

$i =$	1	2	3	4	5	6	7	8
n_1^i	-2.650	2.700	1.556	10.600	0.142	-0.154	0.135	2.720
n_2^i	0.366	0.053	-0.025	0.048	0.043	0.039	0.024	0.375

The negative numbers correspond to sectors where expansion of a sectoral rate of growth would reduce rather than increase the foreign exchange gap or the savings-investment gap. If the structure underlying these results were perfect and if the output of a given sector could be increased solely through the application of additional investment resources, the policy conclusion would be to expand the sectors with negative n-coefficients, provided that the negative coefficient is found for the gap which is the limiting constraint. If that action were taken, the gap would be reduced together with an increased rate of growth of the economy.

In the case of agriculture, clearly, the high negative coefficient does not necessarily warrant such a policy. For one thing, the agricultural sector is probably the most inadequately treated sector in our estimation procedure. Equally important is the fact that application of additional capital in agriculture may not be the decisive factor in increasing agricultural production. Finally, the effect of increased farm output on export proceeds would have to be determined.

The one negative coefficient that certainly is significant is that for the capital-goods-producing sector (sector 3). It is especially significant because, for reasons we shall elaborate on in greater detail in Part 3, there is a strong presumption that the foreign exchange gap will be dominant in 1970 if rates of growth of the economy as high as, or higher than, those implied by key estimate A-1 are attained.

Of all the positive coefficients, once the dominant constraint is determined, the highest should be sought for most efficient utilization of additional resources. If the hypothesis that the foreign exchange gap is dominant is correct, disregarding the rather problematical case of agriculture, the recommendation would then be to expand sector 8 (and most services). Indeed, this sector is likely to impose the least strain on the balance of payments, and thus the greatest increase in national product could be attained from additional foreign resources. This conclusion, however, ought to be understood as an illustration of the method rather than an actual recommendation for Colombia. For any number of reasons the Colombian policy makers may desire to expand sector 8 least of all the sectors.

PART **3** ANALYSIS OF RESULTS

Chapter 6   ECONOMIC THEORY OF THE FOREIGN RESOURCE GAP

6-1   THE NATURE, SIGNIFICANCE, AND DUALITY OF GAP ESTIMATES

Throughout this study we have endeavored to produce two distinct estimates of external resource requirements. Some of the rationale for doing this was given in section 1-2. However, it is only at this stage of the inquiry, having fully developed the projection model, that the significance of the two gaps can be fully understood and the results can be correctly interpreted.

Prima facie there appears to be something inconsistent in producing two different estimates—that of the savings-investment gap and that of the foreign exchange gap—if the two must in the end come out equal to each other. One way of justifying this would be to say that two estimates of the same magnitude could provide a check on the accuracy of the estimation procedure. But this interpretation, while not necessarily incorrect, certainly is not the one underlying the method of this study, nor does it justify the statistical effort required by the dual estimation.

The real significance of the dual procedure lies elsewhere. Valuable information about the character of the development process can be derived from the comparison of the alternative estimates, and what is probably more important, significant policy implications can be derived from that comparison.   Whereas several later sections will be devoted to a fuller elaboration of this notion, at this stage let it be only noted that if, for example, a single gap were considered and it happened that that gap were the smaller of the two, then policies designed to reduce foreign resource requirements through a change in one of the two aggregates determining the particular gap (savings or investment, or alternatively, exports or imports) might turn out to be completely ineffective.   And what is worse, such policies might frustrate the development effort in several respects.

The reason why the two gap evaluations cannot be taken merely as two different estimates of the same statistic is that the actual foreign resource gap, as it eventually will be in reality, is determined by both short- and long-run forces, whereas the gap estimates (as produced in this study) depend only on long-run forces.   There is no reason why the many different long-run determinants should work out exactly into an equality of the two statistics.   This will become especially clear if we realize that entirely different factors and economic agents (decision makers) act upon the four central aggregates—savings, investment, exports, and imports— in the long run.   The savings-investment gap estimate on the one hand and the foreign exchange gap estimate on the other, as produced here, do not have to equal each other in the same sense that *ex ante* savings and investment do not have to be equal in a Keynesian situation.   The analytical difference between the two instances is that in a simple Keynesian model, equality of *ex ante* savings and investment is a sufficient condition of equilibrium, whereas it is not so for an *ex ante* equality between the savings-investment and the foreign exchange gaps.   In the latter situation the equality is a necessary, but not a sufficient, condition.   Sufficiency requires, in addition, the equality of the two gaps to the foreign resources actually forthcoming.

In the context of the subject matter of this study, moreover, the difference is that our concern is not so much with the condition of equilibrium as with a correct estimation of necessary foreign resources, with the level of income and its rate of growth *ex hypothesi* given.   We only have to make sure that the short-run adjustment which in the end will bring to equality the two gaps does not in any way violate the very assumptions whereon the estimates are based, and specifically, that it does not frustrate the overall and sectoral growths assumed.

A condition that will guarantee the actual realization of the rates of growth assumed is that the foreign resources be as large as the larger of the two gaps estimated.   Thus, the larger of the two gaps becomes an estimate of foreign resource requirements consistent with the overall and sectoral rates of growth.   Whether the condition just stated is actually a necessary condition, that is, whether the foreign resource requirements thus estimated are the minimum consistent requirements, must be judged by considering the gap estimates and the whole estimation structure in greater detail.   It is the minimum consistent foreign resource requirements that must be taken as *the* final result (or results, because we are considering a number of alternative growth rates and growth structures) of this study.   In the rest of this section we shall turn to some of the considerations relevant in evaluating the minimum consistent foreign requirements, and we shall turn to others, under separate headings, in some of the following sections.

The key issue may be illustrated by an example.   Suppose that the estimated import-export gap is dominant and equal to $100 million, the other gap being negligible.   If imports entering the dominant gap were only imports of raw materials and investment goods and there were no domestically produced consumer goods readily exportable, then the figure of $100 million is the minimum consistent foreign resource requirement, and hence should be taken as the final estimate for the purposes of this study.   If, however, out of that sum ($100 million) 10 million represent imports of nonessential consumer goods or services that could be eliminated by an appropriate commercial policy without serious political or social repercussions, then the "hard" gap really only is $90 million, and that figure ought to be taken as the minimum consistent requirement.

It is apparent from the example that the crucial problem is one of compressibility.   Given the overall rate of growth and the development structure postulated for the projection period (say 10 years), total investment and imports of capital and intermediate goods and services are inelastic or noncompressible.   Likewise, exports of domestic capital or intermediate goods cannot be expanded in the short run without frustrating development.   All these inelasticities are of purely technological character; change in any one of the aggregates or subaggregates mentioned would always necessitate an alteration of the development process somewhere in the economy, either for lack of capital goods or for lack of intermediate products.

The only instances where such a technological conflict is absent are savings, imports of consumer goods, and exports of consumer goods. But there can be other conflicts—social, political, institutional, and such conflicts (in respect to exports) as are entirely out of reach of the developing countries themselves—limiting alterations of these aggregates. Such limitations (together with the technological limitations mentioned above) then complete the explanation of the incompressibility—or "hardness"—of the two gaps.   Suppose that our previous example is altered, the savings-investment gap being $200 million, and that there is no way of increasing savings above the estimated level. Either—as it often is the case in less developed countries—additional institutions and other means for collecting additional savings are entirely absent or human hardships from further reductions of disposable income would be so great that increasing savings would (or could) lead to development-frustrating political disturbances. Or, alternatively, savings could be forcedly extracted only at prohibitively high costs in terms of limitations of fundamental civil rights. Whatever the case may be, with incompressible savings and growth-determined investment, the "hard" dominant gap is $200 million, and the consistent minimum requirement is equal to that figure.

If the dominant estimated requirement (such as the estimates produced in this study thus far) is found to be only the "consistent," and not "minimum consistent" requirement, then it must be ascertained that the corresponding minimum is not smaller than the other estimated gap. If it were smaller, then the process of finding the minimum must be applied to the estimate which originally was found to be smaller. Using subscript m to indicate a minimum consistent estimate, we can illustrate this situation by the following example: $IS = 200$, $ME = 170$, and $IS_m = 150$. If then the import-export gap is found incompressible, that is, if $ME = ME_m$, that gap is now dominant and the minimum consistent foreign requirement is 170.

6-2 CONSISTENT REQUIREMENTS, CONSISTENT MINIMUM REQUIREMENTS, AND THE *EX POST* ADJUSTMENT OF GAPS

Suppose now that the minimum requirement F_m consistent with the assumed rates of development is determined from the dominant minimum gap (namely, IS_m or ME_m, whichever is larger). The minimum requirement F_m must be forthcoming in the projection period, for if it were not, the underlying growth structure and rate of growth could never be realized. But availability of F_m is only a necessary, and not a sufficient, condition of the assumed growth rates. Whether the preassigned growth structure is realized will also depend on the process of short-run *ex post* adjustment of the two gaps to F_m.

Two types of adjustment must be considered: (1) adjustment from the estimated to the minimum dominant gap, that is, to F_m, and (2) adjustment of the smaller minimum gap to the larger (dominant) minimum gap.

The first type of adjustment does not call for an extensive discussion. Indeed, if the dominant estimated gap is found to be different from the minimum gap, then the very reasoning that leads to the establishment of the minimum gap from the estimated gap must also contain a full description of the process of adjustment.   For example, a postulate of $IS = 200$ and $IS_m = 150$ must be based on an argument such that there is additional flexibility in the tax structure, over and above the tax structure underlying (or implicit in) the estimated savings function.   Such an additional flexibility then must be tapped through appropriate policy measures in order to attain the minimum gap.   Note that if this were not done and only the minimum consistent requirement of 150 were available from foreign sources, the autonomous—non-policy-induced—adjustment could have adverse effects òn development.   For example, with the implied excess of 50 of effective demand over available resources, inflation could result (or could be increased), further discouraging savings, and the investors might not be able to raise enough capital to finance the volume of investment called for by the assumed growth rates.

This being said, let us now turn to the second type of adjustment.   To isolate the first from the second type of adjustment and to make our analysis simple, let us assume that both the estimated gaps are also the minimum gaps, so that the dominant estimated gap indicates the magnitude of F_m.   In the limiting case where

$$IS = ME = F_m \qquad\qquad (6\text{-}1)$$

of course, no adjustment is necessary.   The two situations that concern us are

$$IS < ME = F_m \qquad\qquad (6\text{-}2)$$
$$ME < IS = F_m \qquad\qquad (6\text{-}3)$$

In relation (6-2)—with F_m necessarily forthcoming—the appropriate course of action is to reduce savings; this can be done most readily through reduced taxation of one kind or another.   Secondary economic targets, such as existence of excess stocks or of excess capacities in the economy, can provide an additional criterion for selective tax reductions.

An inappropriate policy would be to try to further stimulate productive investment.   First, this would vitiate the underlying growth assumptions, and second and more important, import requirements would be liable to increase.   In fact, whenever investment projects cannot be undertaken without some foreign inputs, it is impossible to adjust the IS gap to the dominant gap through increased investment.

Finally, let us briefly consider the very real situation where the authorities of the developing country, while receiving the minimum consistent requirements F_m, neglect the gap disparity altogether and rely entirely on autonomous economic adjustment, that is, on adjustment through free market forces.   If prices are inflexible in the downward direction—or if, as the case may often be, rigid inflationary trends prevail—undesired

inventories can accumulate.   This in turn will generally result in a reduction in economic activity and excess of existing capacity, or in a reduced
impetus to invest.   Such tendencies, it is true, will generally reduce the
foreign resource requirements.   But it will be noted that whether through
less than full employment of existing capacity or through deficient capital
formation, economic development is bound to suffer.

Even if prices were perfectly flexible, or if prevailing inflationary trends
could readily respond to deficiencies of effective demand, the situation
implied by relation (6-2) without policy interference could affect entre-
preneurs' confidence and expectations and thus could lead again to a
reduced investment effort and a decline in the overall rate of growth.

Consider now the second alternative, that is, relation (6-3).   The
savings-investment gap is now dominant (binding) and determines the
minimum consistent requirement of foreign resources.   Again assuming
that F_m is forthcoming, the proper policy now is to relax import restrictions on nonessential—presumably mostly consumer—products.   If the
market for foreign exchanges were perfectly unimpeded (as might be the
case in some exceptional situations involving very underdeveloped countries with some abundant natural resource) a case could even be made for
a currency appreciation or for a reduction in import duties.   Alternatively, exports of some products that could be readily consumed at home
could be reduced through an appropriate policy measure.

If imports of capital goods and intermediate products are controlled
along with other imports, that is, if the desired (assumed) rate of capital
formation and growth is controlled, among other measures, through
quantitative restrictions and/or exchange controls, then a relaxation of
such controls would be undesirable.   It would lead (at least in the short
run) to an increased investment; and thus the binding gap would be
increased, and F_m would fall short of the minimum requirement consistent with increased capital formation and growth.

The neglect of the gap disparity and reliance on autonomous forces of
adjustment by the authorities again appear undesirable, although perhaps
less so than it was in relation (6-2).   The situation now is reversed.
With an excess of the *ex ante* savings-investment gap over the import-
export gap there will be an excess of effective demand over effective supply
in the economy,[1] and either undesired inventory decumulation or infla-

---

[1] To illustrate this by an example, suppose that an economy whose net national
product in the projection period is 1,000, necessary investment 200, necessary imports
150 (with only capital goods being imported), maximum savings 100, and possible
exports 100.   For simplicity assume that there is no domestic demand for export
products.   With 50 of capital goods and services being produced domestically, supply
of consumer goods and services must be 850.   However, demand for such goods and
services is 900, that is, net national product minus savings.

tionary pressures will have to produce the *ex post* adjustment.   In the former case total *ex post* investment will be smaller than the intended or necessary (i.e., necessary to generate the assumed rate of growth) investment according to the amount of involuntary inventory decumulation. Thus, in fact, the adjustment will take place via a reduction in the (dominant) savings-investment gap to the level of the other gap.   The growth process still will not be vitiated because the productive (or growth) investment will have been realized.   However, with a reduced demand for investment credit and a reduced savings-investment gap, the decumulation of inventories will be matched by an equivalent accumulation of foreign exchange.   Actually, it is this amount of foreign exchange that would permit—under the above recommended policy of import liberalization—the replenishment of inventories to a normal level from foreign sources.

Of course, the adjustment just discussed could never be lasting.   In the long run, with limited inventories, market forces would necessarily lead to inflation.   This in turn would tend to reduce exports either through a transfer of productive resources or from increased competition by domestic buyers.   And thus, the temporarily accumulated foreign exchange reserves would tend to return to their original level, and the export-import gap would tend to adjust to the (initially larger) savings-investment gap.   However, such an adjustment would be produced through a trade contraction rather than through a trade expansion. Note that with the policy of import liberalization trade would have been expanded, whereas in the absence of any policy exports would be contracted.   In fact, with rising prices not only would exports have been reduced but the importers' rent (or quasi rent) with unchanged import prices would have grown.   And this is equivalent, from the point of view of efficiency of resource allocation, to increased commercial protection—definitely undesirable from the point of view of world welfare, and also undesirable for most less developed countries.

6-3   EMPIRICAL TESTS OF GAP DOMINANCE

Although it is easier to discuss dominance of one gap over another in the context of theoretical, *ex ante* analysis—as we have done thus far—it is not entirely impossible to acquire some knowledge as to whether one or the other gap is dominant from (*ex post*) observation of concrete situations.   Some of the rationale of empirical testing for gap dominance is contained implicitly in the preceding two sections.   These pieces of analysis we shall use here in arriving at a set of objective tests.

Suppose first that a situation is observed where just about all imports are capital goods together with intermediate goods and services, and no important quantities of exportable consumer goods are consumed domestically. From that situation we can learn two things: (1) The foreign resources forthcoming—that is, the current balance of payments deficit (it could on the limit be zero, or there could be a surplus)—are the minimum consistent requirement F_m; (2) the import-export gap is dominant or, on the limit, equal to the investment-savings gap. The "minimum consistent" should now be interpreted as minimum consistent with the rate of growth and structure actually observed.

Observe that if either imports were further contracted or exports of development goods were further expanded—so that the ME gap were reduced—the rate of expansion of the economy would have to drop below that actually observed. It may also be useful to point out now, in relation to a concrete situation, one of the policy arguments stated in the preceding section. Suppose that the current inflow of foreign resources F_m is all that the less developed country can hope for in the near future. Suppose also that the observed savings rate is relatively low and that, as a result, the authorities decide to try to stimulate growth through increased savings, via taxation. Such additional domestic resources then must be channeled either directly or through the banking system into the capital market. Except in the most unlikely situation where some investment projects can be found not requiring foreign capital goods and/or intermediate products, that policy cannot lead to any stimulation of economic growth. On the contrary, because some purchasing power is now withdrawn from the consumers, there is a prospect for depression and less than full capacity utilization in some sectors of the economy.

In fact, the only viable policy that can raise the rate of expansion, in the situation discussed here, in the short or intermediate run is the acquisition of additional foreign resources. In the long run, of course, the development pattern could be redesigned in the direction of an increased substitution for imports of capital and intermediate goods, and a production of additional exportables. Note, however, that this course may in some instances be quite difficult, and on the limit impossible. Foreign markets may offer only limited opportunities, or opportunities at the cost of deteriorating terms of trade. Even expansion of imported competing industries may call for additional imports of raw and intermediate products. But the most important hindrance—especially for smaller countries—can prove to be the diseconomies and extreme inefficiency of small-scale operation. The industries most subject to such impediments, unfortunately, generally happen to be the most important for the development effort, including manufacture of machinery and equipment as well as natural resource industries.

Turning now to the second alternative, suppose that we observe for a particular developing country substantial imports of nondevelopmental goods and services and/or sizable internal consumption of products that could readily be exported without significant adverse price (terms-of-trade) effects. What can we conclude? First, we can be sure that the savings-investment gap is dominant. Indeed, with increased savings (and if necessary, with selective fiscal measures) imports of nondevelopmental goods and services could be reduced and/or exports of such goods and services could be increased without hampering development. But can we say—as we did in the preceding situation—that the foreign resources currently forthcoming actually are minimum consistent, that is, F_m? The evidence assumed does not justify that conclusion, except if we want to adopt a very broad definition of feasibility, that is, if we say that the actual savings are also maximum savings, because the political and economic forces determining savings just do not permit any higher savings rate. Otherwise, to answer our second question, it would be necessary to undertake a fairly careful study of savings behavior and of some relevant institutional factors.

While it is impossible to ascertain from purely economic evidence whether the dominant IS gap is also a minimum gap, that is, whether the observed F is also F_m, it is now possible—contrary to the first situation—to evaluate the degree of dominance of the IS gap over the ME gap. For example, an adequate index of dominance would be the sum of nondevelopmental imports of goods and services and the internal consumption of nonessential exportables divided by the observed (*ex post*) gap. The higher the index is, the stronger the dominance of the savings-investment gap over the other gap. If the index is equal to zero, or very close to it, we are facing the other situation: dominance of ME over IS.

However, the index cannot tell us how strongly the ME gap is dominant over the IS gap, because the index remains zero whenever that relationship prevails. The reason why we can evaluate at least approximately the degree of dominance in one case and not in the other is that it is possible to identify the type of imports of consumption without which development could continue largely undisturbed, while it is impossible to identify dollars that could have been saved and were not. If, in the latter situation, savings were found quite low, well below some average savings rate realized in the past, then, perhaps, it could be argued that the dollars that could have been saved and were not are indicated by the difference between the currently observed and the maximum past-observed average savings rates. Or, alternatively, that difference could be taken as indicative of the lower limit of the magnitude sought.

What we have discussed thus far we may term a set of statistical—or, alternatively, equilibrium—tests. However, it ought to be noted in concluding this section that other tests may be available. From the nature of dynamic disequilibria, such as inflationary or deflationary tendencies, utilization of capacity, trends in inventory formation, foreign exchange reserves, short-term capital flows, and other disequilibria, a well-advised economist can conclude a good deal. Since we do not go into this subject here, let it only be indicated that some of the policy alternatives discussed in the preceding section provide a useful, though by no means complete, set of tools for such an analysis.

A dynamic phenomenon strongly suggesting the dominance of the import-export gap is the impact of terms-of-trade variation on the average savings rate which we have established in Chapter 3. We do not elaborate on this important subject here, however, because all Chapter 8 is devoted to it.

6-4   THE FOREIGN RESOURCE GAP AND THE THEORY OF FOREIGN EXCHANGES

The standing theory of foreign exchanges, including its very recent developments, appears most inadequate to explain the conditions prevailing in the foreign exchange markets of developing countries. This situation would not have to concern us, and we could pass over it, were it not for the fact that the essence of this entire study negates some of the fundamentals of the traditional theory. Although a considerable body of literature has developed on questions of stability and multiplicity of market equilibria, the problem of a possible absence of any equilibrium solution in the foreign exchange market has scarcely ever been examined in a formal fashion. And yet, note that if the existence of an equilibrium in the foreign exchange market (corresponding to autonomous transactions) were always guaranteed, the very foundations of this study would have to crumble and any effort to estimate foreign resource requirements of developing countries would be quite meaningless.[2]

A comprehensive analysis of the problem—or set of problems—just raised would require far more effort and space than can be devoted to it here. Consequently, we have to limit ourselves to a brief—and sometimes not quite rigorous—exposition of principal points.

Let us first state the crux of the dilemma. A given invariant structure of the economy whose foreign exchange market is studied is the basic assumption of the standing theory of foreign exchanges. It is most often

[2] It is certainly not the philosophy of our foreign aid program to give aid for the sole reason of safeguarding the recipient countries from the hardships that would be caused by currency depreciation.

a tacit assumption in more traditional analyses, and it is quite explicit in recent writings.   In the context of the present study, the assumption can be translated into the assumption of a zero rate of growth.   We have not stated that a savings-investment gap or an export-import gap could be present in a completely stagnant economy for any and all exchange rates.   What we do claim is that for some positive high enough rate of growth of a less developed country, and for a given low enough time horizon (that is, we eliminate the case where the foreign exchange market schedules—supply and demand—correspond to a "long run" of, say, 50 years or more, a case which is anyway meaningless for the present analysis), no equality of exports and imports on current account will be attainable, whatever the rate of exchange, demand for foreign exchange being always greater than the supply of it.

As a first approximation, the situation is illustrated in Figure 6.   In ED_0 we recognize the customary excess demand for foreign exchange corresponding to a zero rate of growth.   The equilibrium in the foreign exchange market—that is, $ED = 0$—is found at the point e, for R equal to the distance between the origin and e.   As the rate of growth of the economy is required to increase from zero to, say 2, 4, and 6 per cent per annum, we obtain excess demand functions ED_1, ED_2, and ED_3 respectively.   For ED_2 and ED_3, it will be noted, no equilibrium solution (intersection with the vertical axis) exists.

Before proceeding to a more detailed analysis of the case, some general remarks must be made regarding the characteristics and underlying

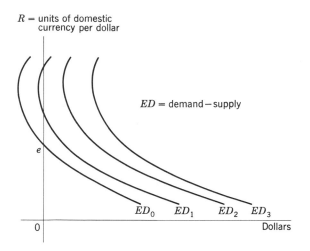

Figure 6.   Excess demand curves in the foreign exchange market of a less developed economy corresponding to various rates of growth.

assumptions of the excess demand functions.   First it will be observed that these functions correspond to what we might term an "intermediate run" (in the Marshallian sense) of, say, five years or a somewhat longer period.   Second, the usual assumption is made that everyone is permitted to trade in the foreign exchange market absolutely freely.   Third, and most important, the public authorities are postulated to engage in policies—such as fiscal, monetary, credit, or any other policy—to generate (1) the required overall rate of growth (such as the 0, 2, 4, or 6 per cent in our example) and (2) an adequate, or (to the extent it is possible or definable) an optimal, development structure.[3]

To assume a given policy or set of policies is not as unusual as might appear at first.   Note that even in the context of traditional analysis of the foreign exchange market where a zero rate of growth is implicitly or explicitly postulated, the foreign exchange market schedules are not at all defined, or definable, unless definite assumptions are made regarding the monetary policy engaged in by the authorities.[4]   Also it will be noted that a given policy mix must be assumed if we want to speak about alternative rates of growth because under conditions of a perfect *laissez faire* there could generally be only one "equilibrium" rate of economic growth (a very low rate, indeed, for most less developed countries).

But let us now turn to a more careful consideration of the various factors underlying the situations depicted in Figure 6.   There are several sets of categories relevant for our discussion.   First of all, we have to discuss the supply and demand for foreign exchange separately.   Second, we have to bring into our discussion the dichotomy between the savings-investment gap on the one hand and the export-import gap on the other.   Third, conditions of supply and demand of goods and services internationally traded must be considered separately.   Fourth, and finally, we have to use the distinction between essential (or development) goods and services and the nondevelopmental goods and services entering international exchange.

Let us first turn to the demand side of the foreign exchange market. It will be recalled that the demand for foreign exchange we talk about is *autonomous* free demand for exchange to be used for transactions in goods and services.   That demand is derived from the demand for, and supply of, imports of goods and services.   It can safely be assumed that the supply of imports is infinitely elastic, that is, the less developed

[3] Note that if, in the extreme, the government is engaged in a policy of generating real growth exclusively through an expansion of government services, the excess demand for foreign exchange might not move at all to the right for higher rates of growth of the gross national product.

[4] One customary assumption, also implicit in our later discussion, is that the supply of money remains proportional to real income.

country cannot affect the world price (expressed in foreign exchange) of its import products.   Under such conditions the elasticity of demand for foreign exchange is equal to the elasticity of demand for imports. Similarly, if the import market is subdivided into alternative segments according to type of transaction, the elasticity of demand for foreign exchange in each segment is equal to the elasticity of demand for imports of the particular variety.

Now two types of imports of goods and services must be distinguished: (1) imports on account of derived demand, namely, capital goods, raw material, and semifinished products; and (2) imports by consumers, or imports of finished products for consumption.   In the short and intermediate run, demand for the former is very (if not completely) inelastic once the rate of growth is prescribed, and so must be the demand for foreign exchange (assumed dollars) on account of derived demand (development) imports.[5]

This inelasticity—illustrated by D_d in Figure 7—stems primarily from the fact that a prescribed rate of growth calls for a given volume of certain specific goods and services which simply cannot be substituted for from domestic sources in substantial amounts prior to the attainment of a relatively advanced stage of development.   Another reason for such an impossibility of substitution, especially for primary (nonproduced) factors, is the lack of a sufficient number of alternative technologies. Often only one technique is available for a given product or service.

The other component of demand D_c (added to D_d in the diagram) resembles the traditionally postulated demand for foreign exchange; it has a definite nonzero elasticity and, as indicated in Figure 7, may be eliminated completely for a high enough rate of exchange in terms of domestic currency.

The second characteristic of D_c—as suggested—is not a necessary one. Indeed, the demand for consumer goods can be completely eliminated

---

[5] In the long run, of course, a nonzero elasticity can be postulated.   However, even with a span of time of, say, 10 years, the responsiveness of demand for development imports to changes in the rate of exchange may not be very high.   Note for example one of the most promising avenues of import substitution: expansion of capital goods production.   With an increased rate of exchange, foreign capital goods will become more expensive, and thus higher prices could be charged for comparable domestically produced machinery and equipment.   But note that domestic production of machinery often will call for extensive imports of foreign equipment and technical expertise which now also become more expensive (in terms of domestic currency).   Especially in less developed countries where interest rates and internal rates of return generally are high, it is then by no means necessary that either an internal rate-of-return or a present-discounted-value computation would support devaluation of currency as a means of stimulating domestic capital goods industries.   Similar arguments could be offered with regard to imports of raw materials that cannot be supplied domestically at all and with regard to some semimanufactures.

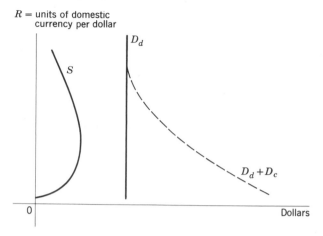

Figure 7.   The two main components of demand for foreign exchange
and supply of foreign exchange in a typical developing
country.

only if the export-import gap is dominant and there is no difficulty of
mobilizing internal savings up to the point consistent with the level of
investment and the (minimum consistent) foreign trade balance. If
this condition is not fulfilled, that is, if the savings-investment gap is
dominant, then the broken line $D_d + D_c$ would have to become vertical
in its upper portion somewhere to the right of D_d. The rationale of this
is that even if the government were to devalue considerably, it would
have to subsidize at least some imports of consumer goods in order to
keep effective savings below a certain maximum level, or, what is the
same thing, to keep consumption above a certain minimum level consistent with the attainment of a prescribed rate of growth.

Of course, if the constraint on savings were a purely institutional one
(for a given rate of exchange), then savings *might* be increased through
devaluation, and thus the savings-investment gap could be reduced.
However, a possible adverse effect must be noted. Suppose that with
a less than infinite elastic demand for exports the terms of trade of the
depreciating country deteriorate; then the real income of the less developed
country would have to decline; and if there is some minimum permissible
level of consumption, the maximum permissible savings would have
to decline. Under such conditions it would definitely be preferable
to eliminate imports of nonessential consumer goods through means other
than devaluation.

To sum up, there is strong evidence that the (free) demand for foreign
exchange of developing countries contains an important component

attributable to the development effort, positively related to the rate of growth and highly or entirely insensitive to variations in the rate of exchange in the short and intermediate run. Using our terminology of the preceding sections, we can identify that component as the minimum demand for foreign exchange consistent with a given rate of growth. What remains of total demand is what we may call a dispensable demand for foreign exchange. That component is generally responsive to rate of exchange variations, and it can be eliminated through a variety of policy actions without impeding development. Elimination through devaluation may not be the most desirable policy. One reason is the possibility of its adversely affecting the level of maximum attainable savings already explained. Another reason is that with very high prices of foreign exchange the very policies that are assumed to guarantee a given rate of growth (defining the demand for foreign exchange) may be rendered cumbersome, if not impossible. For example, with a very high price of foreign exchange and hence of imported capital goods, internal rate-of-return computations might lead to rejection of necessary development projects.

We may now consider briefly the supply side of the foreign exchange market. The usual form of the supply function is indicated by S in Figure 7. By "usual" we mean that the supply of foreign exchange is thus generally represented in traditional analyses of the foreign exchange market. The exact form of the supply curve is really immaterial for our argument. A less developed country may or may not have a supply function such as that in Figure 7. The only thing that is important, and on which the possibility of existence of an incompressible foreign resource gap crucially depends, is that the supply function not have a positive elasticity at all its points. For if that elasticity were always positive, there would have to be some rate of exchange high enough to close the foreign resource gap.

At this point it may be useful to recall that a sufficient condition for a zero elasticity of supply of foreign exchange is either (1) a zero elasticity of supply of exports or (2) a unit elasticity of demand for exports. Note further that the elasticity of supply will be negative (as in the upper portion of S in Figure 7) with either (1) a negative elasticity of supply of exports or (2) a less than unitary elasticity of demand for exports. Observe that even in the weaker case of a zero elasticity the S-curve would be parallel to D_d, and to the extent that S is to the left of D_d, there would be an incompressible foreign resource gap.

Consider first the more straightforward situation where the savings-investment gap is dominant. We assume that the difference between the minimum export-import gap and the minimum savings-investment gap is already adjusted through given imports of consumer goods, so that a zero-elastic demand for foreign exchange, such as D_d in Figure 7, also includes demand for such imports; no other imports except those just mentioned and the derived demand development imports are permitted to enter the country.

Under these conditions, the supply of exports will be zero elastic because no productive resources or products can be withdrawn from domestic use to be exported. And thus also the supply of foreign exchange will be zero elastic. Consequently, devaluation in a developing country experiencing a foreign resource gap dominated by the savings-investment constraint cannot lead to an improvement in the situation.

Now let us turn to the supply of foreign exchange in situations where the savings-investment gap is not dominant, that is, where resources or a surplus of exportable goods and services can—or could—be mobilized. For exporters of primary commodities that control an appreciable share of the world market the elasticity of demand for exports generally will be no greater than unity, and thus, in such situations, the supply of foreign exchange from such exports can hardly have a positive elasticity, whatever the elasticity of supply. For relatively less important exporters of primary products—irrespective of the fact that at least in the short run, supply is likely to be inelastic, which in itself can reduce the foreign exchange elasticity to zero—the low elasticity of total world demand most often will lead to oligopolistic restraint of export volume, either tacit or embodied in a commodity agreement of one form or another. And thus, a positive elasticity of supply of foreign exchange is again unlikely. Even in the most favorable situation of oil exports, the elasticity of supply of foreign exchange will not be high, in spite of a high elasticity of demand, because the fraction of domestic factor inputs whose cost is not directly affected by exchange-rate variation is often very small. Thus on account of the (by far) most significant export of less developed countries—primary commodities—a zero elasticity of the supply of foreign exchange appears to be a very likely hypothesis.

With respect to the remaining type of exports of manufactured products, at present quite unimportant for most less developed countries, one favorable factor must be recognized: the elasticities of supply of exports certainly are not anywhere near zero. Actually, they may be quite high, infinite, or even very large and negative on account of increasing returns in such industries. Consequently, zero or negative elasticity of supply of foreign exchange cannot be argued on grounds of inelastic export supplies.[6] The difficulty here generally lies with the elasticity of demand for exports, and with the unhappy "mathematical reality" that

---

[6] Recall that this statement pertains only to the class of situations where the savings-investment gap is not dominant.

it takes only a unit elasticity of demand for exports to get a zero-elastic supply of foreign exchange.

Now the inelasticity of advanced countries' demand for exports of nonprimary products from the less developed countries is a very real thing, and hardly any important exceptions to that rule can be found. Part of the explanation is to be found with institutional or policy factors, part with the very nature of economic forces determining the demand in question. Turning first to the latter, it will be noted that for most manufactures markets in the advanced countries are highly differentiated. The degree of substitutability between a less developed country's product and another product of the same denomination generally is low, and this is sufficient to render the elasticity of demand for less developed countries' produce low. The differentiation sometimes derives from prejudice, sometimes from reality because of inferior craftsmanship or differences of taste and design.

As we proceed from finished manufactures toward less and less highly fabricated goods, it is true, the degree of product and market differentiation diminishes. However, at this point the institutional, or policy, factor comes in; it leads in a vast majority of cases to quantitative restrictions, high tariffs, and other—often more subtle—forms of import control on the part of the advanced countries. If the restrictions are quantitative, the elasticity of demand is zero, and in consequence the elasticity of supply of foreign exchange significantly negative. Such a negative component generally will then outweigh positive elasticities possibly present with respect to some other segments of the export market.

In the introduction to this section we pointed out the complexity of the subject dealt with here and also stated that, consequently, the analysis could not be very rigorous. At least one such imperfection—or lack of rigor—must be considered before we leave the subject, and its bearing on our main conclusions must be briefly examined. In order to assimilate our analysis to the traditional treatment of the foreign exchange market (in a static economy), we have postulated for a given assumed rate of growth a single excess demand for foreign exchange and a single set of supply and demand functions. To minimize the biases that could arise from that postulate, we spoke about short- or intermediate-run relationships. Indeed, over shorter periods of time the shifts in the schedules resulting from the growth of the economy could not be very significant.

However, over longer periods, such as the 10- to 15-year projection periods considered earlier in this study, it is inadmissible to speak of a single set of supply and demand functions, corresponding to a given rate of growth, for the entire period. The excess demand for foreign exchange must be expected to travel in one direction or another as the economy is expanding.   At the same time, as longer and longer periods are considered, longer-run schedules must be visualized, with, presumably, higher elasticities on account of a longer adjustment period.

The full implication of the dynamic forces involved here can be discussed with reference to Figure 8.   Suppose that ED_3 is a three-year intermediate-run excess demand function in the foreign exchange market of the type we have discussed until now.   It represents only the dominant minimum consistent gap corresponding to a given rate of growth.   There is no other excess demand, dispensable transactions

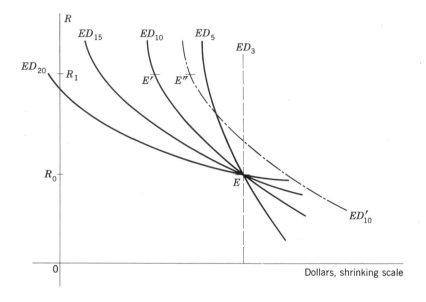

Figure 8.   The effect of the period of adjustment on the foreign exchange market of less developed economies.

having been eliminated through appropriate policies.   The same curve can also be taken as a long-run (minimum) excess demand for foreign exchange provided that the savings-investment gap is, and will remain, dominant throughout the period considered.   Note that in this situation the curve must be perfectly inelastic (or must shift with the size of the dominant savings-investment gap) irrespective of the usual market forces governing the market of foreign exchanges.   This being so, we can now concern ourselves exclusively with the situation where the export-import gap is dominant, and consequently there may be leeway for adjustment in the long run.

The exchange rate R_0, defined here as an index with respect to overall internal price level, is an initial rate of exchange, at which a minimum consistent gap of R_0E arises. Now the curves ED_5, ED_{10}, etc., represent longer- and longer-run excess demand curves for foreign exchange, it being understood that any point on each particular demand function can be attained, through exchange rate variation, in the number of years indicated by the subscript of ED. As could be expected, higher elasticities correspond to longer time spans, that is, to longer-run functions.

Now, to introduce the rate of growth—the factor we partly omitted in the foregoing discussion—let us assume that the horizontal scale shrinks at a rate $\bar{r}$ equal to the rate of growth of the developing economy. The different excess demand curves, remaining as drawn, now are valid provided that for any given rate of exchange and for the structure underlying any given "run" (5, 10 years, etc.) the whole system—that is, real magnitudes of the general equilibrium of the developing economy (note, not prices)—expands in a homogeneous fashion at a rate $\bar{r}$ per annum and provided that the ED's are matched with correspondingly shrunken scales. Of course, it must also be assumed that foreign demand for exports also grows at that rate.

For example, the distance between R_1 and E' indicates the minimum resource gap after 10 years, corresponding to a devaluation from R_0 to R_1 and measured along a horizontal scale where what was initially \$1 is now \$1 times $(1 + \bar{r})^{10}$. As drawn, the gap would be just about equal to the initial gap with a rate of growth of about 6.2 per cent.

Suppose first that with unchanged price relationships throughout, foreign demand actually does expand at the rate equal to the postulated growth of the economy. The rate of increase in the elasticity of the excess demand curve for foreign exchange then competes, so to speak, with the speed of shrinkage of the horizontal scale. As Figure 8 shows (for ED_{10}), the minimum consistent requirements then can either increase, or decrease, or remain the same over alternative periods. The only thing that can be ascertained—this assertion being the equivalent to the postulate of equilibrium in the traditional "stationary" theory of foreign exchange markets—is that for some long enough period the first factor generally will outdistance the second, and an equilibrium will be reached.[7] This is shown for ED_{20} in the diagram.

Now if foreign demand does not grow *pari passu* with the expansion of the economy, but develops at a slower rate, not even in the very long run must there be an equilibrium for a prescribed rate of growth. It

[7] Observe that this statement is valid only for the class of problems discussed here, that is, dominance of the export-import gap. Indeed, for high enough rates of growth there could never be an equilibrium in the foreign exchange market (corresponding to current transactions) because savings could never attain the level of investment called for by such rates of growth.

can only be said that there must be some maximum rate of growth for which equilibrium will be reached over a prescribed period. As indicated by ED'_{10}, the minimum consistent excess demands will now be drifting to the right and thus will reinforce the impact of the shrinking horizontal scale.

Whereas the structural changes imputable to (real) exchange rate alterations are implied by the elasticities of the various excess demand functions, other structural changes (imputable to changes in technology, factor endowments, and demand conditions) are not. Recall the homogeneity assumption, underlying the postulate of a regularly shrinking scale, which in fact precludes any structural change. However, the effects of autonomous structural changes (not imputable to alterations in the rate of exchange) can now conveniently be studied with the "central" homogeneous state as a point of reference.

Let us consider the three factors of structural change separately. Probably the simplest answer can be given in respect to changes in technology. There seems to be no special reason to believe that this factor would exercise an effect in any direction on the ED functions. The ED functions may shift to the right or to the left, and on balance can be expected to remain unaffected by technical change. Whereas it is true that a special effort may be devoted to improvements of technology in the export- and import-competing industries, it is equally true that new techniques often require more, and more costly, foreign equipment, especially in countries in early stages of development.

The demand factor, both within and without the less developed countries, tends to be an unfavorable one, the income elasticities of typical less developed countries' exports being generally low, and the income elasticities of typical import products generally high. On this account, then, the ED curves can be expected to shift to the right, as indicated already.

Only the changes in factor endowments can, in a special way, brighten the outlook. With relative factor endowments of the less developed countries becoming more like those of the advanced countries, a contraction (relative to the size of the growing economies) of trade between the advanced and less advanced countries could be expected. In terms of our analysis this then can be interpreted as a slowdown of the rate of shrinking of the horizontal axis in Figure 8, below the (prescribed) rate of growth of the developing country $\bar{r}$.

Chapter 7 THE GROSS CAPITAL - OUTPUT COEFFICIENT: ITS USE FOR PREDICTION AND THE BIASES INVOLVED

Paradoxically, the gross capital-output coefficient is one of the most useful (or at least most widely used) and most dubious tools of development analysis and prediction. The only excuse that economists—including the author—have for using it is the impossibility of finding another operational tool for which satisfactory statistical data would be available.

The difficulty with the gross capital-output coefficient resides in its inherent instability. More specifically, it is a questionable procedure to estimate the coefficient from some historical evidence and expect that it will remain unchanged over the period of prediction. With respect to highly aggregative capital-output coefficients, one obvious difficulty derives from changing structures of the developing economy. Unless the capital coefficients are identical in all sectors, a changing structure will generally lead to a change in the aggregate coefficient. In this study we have attempted to at least reduce this type of bias by disaggregating the structure into a limited number of sectors.

Another basic difficulty is a possibility of changing technology, or that of factor substitution. Given the present state of economic science and economists' knowledge of technology in less developed countries, however, very little can be done about this aspect of the problem. It can only be hypothesized that if the period over which predictions are sought is sufficiently short (say, not exceeding the periods considered in the empirical part of this study), a given volume of additional output (national or sectoral) will require a proportional increase in total capital stock, the factor of proportionality between increments in output and net capital formation being at least approximately unchanged. The rationale behind this notion (especially for the less developed countries) is either that technology is subject to fixed coefficients and labor really is not a scarce factor; or that if capital-labor substitution actually takes place, the law of diminishing (marginal) returns is offset by gradual increases in total productivity, that is, by improvements in technology; or that both factors cooperate in producing a comparative stability of the net capital-output coefficient.

Unfortunately, a net coefficient generally is not used, for reasons of a virtual impossibility of estimating it. Whereas more or less satisfactory data generally are obtainable for gross capital formation, estimates of net capital formation—or, alternatively, of actual capital consumption and/or replacement—generally are unavailable, and even in the few cases where such estimates were produced, they are necessarily of rather poor quality.

The two principal purposes of this section are (1) to show the biases inherent in using a gross capital-output coefficient for prediction of future investment needs and (2) to derive from that analysis at least an approximate evaluation of the order of magnitude of errors involved in particular situations of prediction. This analysis then will be useful to us in Chapter 9 in making a final appraisal of the empirical results of this study.

Before turning to a rigorous quantitative analysis, let us first consider the essence of the problem. Let us assume that the net capital-output coefficient is constant and call it K_0. Then, assuming a constant period during which capital assets can be used (before they are scrapped and replaced), the gross capital-output coefficient K_i will vary inversely with the rate of growth of the economy (or a particular economic sector) r_i. Such a variation is illustrated in Figure 9. Along the horizontal axis we measure various levels of capital-output coefficients, and along the vertical axis the rates of growth of the economic aggregate under consideration. The solid hyperbola-like curve passing through a and b indicates the relation between r and K on the assumption that a long period of time (strictly speaking, an infinitely long period) is allowed for the growth process to reach a state of dynamic equilibrium. As indicated by the (broken) asymptotes, K becomes infinitely large when the economy is growing at a zero rate, and approaches K_0, the net capital-output coefficient, for very high rates of growth. Whereas the latter situation is of very little practical importance, actual rates of growth never coming close to infinity, the former case is quite real and illustrates in the extreme the point being made. It is quite clear that with a zero rate of growth continuing over long periods of time, some replacement (i.e., gross investment) must be taking place and thus the gross capital coefficient will be infinitely large.

For negative rates of growth, the gross coefficients are indicated by the broken line in the third quadrant of Figure 9. This relation can be analytically defined; however, for the practical purpose of the present study it is of very little relevance and consequently we shall not elaborate on it.

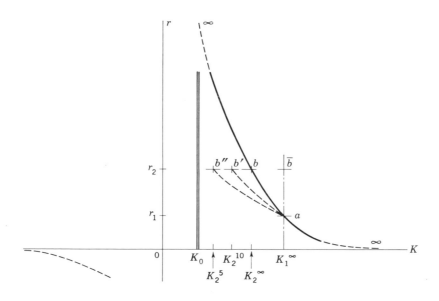

Figure 9.   The relation between the gross capital coefficient and the rate of growth.

Turning back to nonnegative rates of growth, suppose that the production aggregate is growing for a long period at the rate r_1 and consequently that the corresponding gross capital-output coefficient is K_1^∞ (∞ indicating the length of the period). The standard practice is to use the observed coefficient K_1^∞ for prediction as a parameter invariant with respect to the rate of growth. For example, if the rate of growth in the future is to be augmented from the historical level r_1 to a prospective level r_2, then K_1^∞ still will be used for prediction of future gross investment requirements.   And yet it is clear from the diagram that this will imply an error equal to the length of the segment $b\bar{b}$ provided that the projection period is sufficiently long, that is, provided that the year for which investment requirements are to be estimated is sufficiently far in the future.[1]

To relate our exposition to a subsequent mathematical analysis, it is convenient to design at this stage an index of what we may call *long-range bias* B_1, namely,

$$B_1 = \frac{K_1^\infty - K_2^\infty}{K_1^\infty} \qquad\qquad (7\text{-}1)$$

It expresses the magnitude of the bias $b\bar{b}$ as a fraction of the observed coefficient K_1^∞.   A positive B_1 indicates an overestimation of the true future capital-output coefficient, and a negative B_1 an underestimation. Observe that the latter case will arise if the rate of growth is expected to decline in the future.

It is now apparent from the diagram that the lower the rate of growth in the period for which K was observed, the greater is the bias, and hence the greater is the likely error in estimating future gross investment requirements using an observed K for a period of prospective increased rate of expansion.

Of greater practical importance is another type of bias that we may refer to as the *short-range bias*.   Observe that if K_1^∞ is observed over a sufficiently long period and is employed in predicting gross investment for a future year which is, say, only 10 years ahead, in addition to the bias just discussed there will be another source of error of estimation resulting from the fact that in the projection year the growth structure could not have yet adjusted to long-range conditions.   Specifically, the gross coefficient will be even smaller (for an assumed future rate r_2) than K_2^∞, owing to the fact that in 10 years all or most of the net real asset formation that was generating an increased rate of growth will not yet need to be replaced.   For a 10-year projection period—such as that used in this study—the relevant correct capital-output coefficient will be K_2^{10} corresponding to b'.   A hypothetical point b'' indicates the correct capital-output coefficient for a five-year horizon.   The broken lines connecting a with b' and b'' indicate similar conditions for rates of growth between r_1 and r_2.

---

[1] Admittedly, projection horizons as long as to lead to a point such as b are rather unrealistic in the context of any concrete analysis.   However, for purposes of exposition it is important to treat the biases involved in this particular way.

We are now in a position to define another index, that for the short-range bias B_2, as

$$B_2{}^j = \frac{K_1{}^\infty - K_2{}^j}{K_1{}^\infty} \qquad (7\text{-}2)$$

It is apparent that B_1 now becomes only a special case of $B_2{}^j$, for $j = \infty$, that is,

$$B_1 = B_2{}^\infty \qquad (7\text{-}3)$$

It is thus possible to drop the subscript and speak of only one index of bias B^j, where j indicates the number of years to elapse between the base period (period for which the capital coefficient was estimated and from which the projection is being made) and the projection year.

One convenient property of B^j ought to be pointed out. Because in all the elements appearing on the right-hand side of relation (7-2) there appears as a denominator the (assumed) increment in income or product in the projection year, B^j also indicates the bias of estimate of future gross investment. Specifically, B^j also shows the overestimate or underestimate of gross investment in the projection year as a fraction of the (biased) evaluation of investment based on a constant capital-output coefficient such as $K_1{}^\infty$.

A third possible source of error of estimate of future gross investments ought to be briefly discussed before we turn to the quantitative analysis. It has been assumed thus far that the estimate of the gross capital-output coefficient, obtained from historical data, for a historical rate of growth r_1, actually tends to fall on the contour passing through a and b; that is, it has been assumed that the estimate of $K_1{}^\infty$ is unbiased. This by no means has to be the case. Without going into an involved probabilistic analysis, the following intuitive (and rather approximate) propositions can be made.

If, even with short-run fluctuations in the rate of growth of the relevant production aggregate, the overall (average) rate of growth during the period of observation (sample period) was not significantly different from the average rate of growth in the period preceding the period of observation, then the estimate of the gross coefficient can be expected to be an unbiased estimate of the true coefficient corresponding to the historically observed rate of growth. If, however, an acceleration (deceleration) occurred during the sample period over the preceding period, it can be expected that the observed coefficient is an underestimate (overestimate) of the true coefficient corresponding to the historically observed rate of growth during the sample period.

The latter proposition can be better understood by referring again to Figure 9. Suppose that preceding the sample period (say 10 years) the rate of growth was r_1, whereas during the sample period it was r_2. Then the cluster of (10) points representing year-to-year capital coefficients for the sample period will be centered somewhere around b'' rather than around b. And consequently, the estimate of the capital coefficient will tend to be somewhere near $K_2{}^5$ rather than somewhere near $K_2{}^\infty$.

Because it is virtually hopeless to try to obtain data that would be necessary in evaluating the third type of bias, we have to neglect the subject, unfortunately, in our analysis. However, some further general remarks will be very useful. As is apparent from our illustration, the third type of bias involves a (possible) deviation from the long-range curve passing through a and b, but not a deviation from $\bar{b}$ as did both the first and second types of bias discussed. In other words, the third bias is comparable in both nature and magnitude to the difference between the second and the first types of bias. In simple terms, the errors that *may* arise in estimating future gross investment from imperfect estimation of a long-range coefficient (such as $K_1{}^\infty$) are commensurate with the difference between (previously defined) B_2 and B_1. And as will be shown later in this section, such a difference can very often be expected to be quite small.

Turning now to the quantitative analysis, let us assume that an unbiased estimate of $K_1{}^\infty$ is obtained for the rate of growth r_1, and let us take it to be a given number K_1 (say, four). Assuming further that all capital goods have to be replaced after A years, it is easily established that the net capital-output coefficient K_0 is

$$K_0 = K_1 \left[1 - \frac{1}{(1 + r_1)^A} \right] \tag{7-4}$$

Thus an estimate of K_1 and an estimate of A lead to an estimate of K_0, the net capital-output coefficient assumed to be invariant with respect to the rate of growth, with respect to the replacement period—and, in fact, for our purpose, with respect to time. With K_0 a constant and with K and r able to assume any values, relation (7-4) now becomes the function described by the line passing through a and b in Figure 9.

The index A is a parameter which must be obtained independently from the procedure discussed here. Although its precise meaning is the replacement period assumed equal for all productive assets, it can be approximated by an average replacement period. If it is impossible to estimate A with any degree of satisfactory accuracy, relation (7-4) at least enables us to study the first bias (explained above) for given ranges of the period A.

The index of long-range bias B^∞ now can easily be obtained using relation (7-4), namely,

$$B^\infty = 1 - \frac{1 - 1/(1 + r_1)^A}{1 - 1/(1 + r_2)^A} \tag{7-5}$$

where, we recall, A is the (average) replacement period, r_1 the observed rate of growth for which K_1^∞ was estimated, and r_2 the rate of growth postulated for the projection period.

To give a concrete example and to make quite clear the interpretation of the index, suppose that the replacement period A is 20 years and that the rate of growth r_1 observed over the past period for which the coefficient K_1 was estimated is 0.04. If now an estimate of investment is sought for a period very far in the future, using the observed coefficient K_1 and assuming that the future rate of growth will be $r_2 = 0.06$, the investment estimate obtained will be about 19 per cent[2] higher than the correct estimate which would have been obtained if K_2 (corresponding to 6 per cent rate of growth) were used. As is explained above, this statement is equivalent to saying that B^∞ is equal to 0.19, or that K_2^∞ is 81 per cent of K_1^∞.

The evaluation of the index of short-range bias B^j (with finite j) is a good deal more involved than that just presented for long projection periods. However, it becomes quite manageable if the assumption is made that j never exceeds A, that is, that the projection period is no longer than the (average) replacement period. For calculations of the type presented earlier in this study, with horizons of 10 or at most 15 years, this assumption is highly realistic. Hardly ever could it happen that the actual average replacement period computed over *all* capital assets would be as short as 10 years, and only rarely can it be expected to be as low as 15 years. Observe that we speak here of the replacement period and not of the accounting concept of depreciation period, which, indeed, in many less developed countries may be considerably shorter.

For reasons of convenience, let us first consider a number R, defined by

$$1 + r_2 = (1 + r_1)(1 + R) \tag{7-6}$$

As is apparent from relation (7-6), R is the degree of acceleration (or deceleration) of the rate of growth in the projection period, measured from the rate of growth r_1 established for the historical period for which the gross capital coefficient was computed. It will also be apparent from the relation that with both r_1 and r_2 not too large, R will be approximately the difference between r_2 and r_1. Exactly, it follows from relation (7-6) that r_2 is equal to $(r_1 + R + r_1 R)$.

[2] This percentage is measured in terms of the incorrect estimate.

Now suppose that the aggregate studied V has been growing at the rate r_1 through the base period "0" (zero) and that the rate of growth has increased by the factor R thereafter for the future period extending through year j. Under these conditions, it is possible to visualize our aggregate following the base period (zero) decomposed into two parts. The first is growing at the historical rate r_1, and the second is equal to the difference between the aggregate growing at the rate r_2 (or $r_1 + R + r_1R$) and the aggregate growing at the rate r_1. It will be noticed that as long as the replacement period is longer than the projection period ($A > j$), investment necessary to generate the growth of the second component will never have to be replaced during the future period considered.

Using V_0 for the magnitude of the growing aggregate in the base period, the correct expression for total gross investment in (the projection) period j, that is, I_j, thus can be expressed as

$$I_j = K_1V_0 \left\{ (1 + r_1)^{j-1}r_1 \right.$$

$$+ \left[1 - \frac{1}{(1 + r_1)^A} \right] [(1 + r_1 + R + r_1R)^{j-1}(r_1 + R + r_1R)$$

$$\left. - (1 + r_1)^{j-1}r_1] \right\} \quad (7\text{-}7)$$

Note that the coefficient of the second square bracket of relation (7-7) times K_1 (the observed historical coefficient of investment) actually is the constant *net* coefficient K_0.

Now the (incorrect) evaluation of gross investment in period j, that is, $\bar{I}_j$, based on the historical gross capital-output coefficient K_1, is

$$\bar{I}_j = K_1V_0(1 + r_1 + R + r_1R)^{j-1}(r_1 + R + r_1R) \quad (7\text{-}8)$$

Recalling the alternative definitions of the index of short-range bias,

$$B^j = 1 - \frac{I_j}{\bar{I}_j} = 1 - \frac{K_2{}^j}{K_1} \quad (7\text{-}9)$$

(note that the superscript ∞ is omitted with K_1) that index can be obtained from relations (7-7) and (7-8). After a few simplifying operations, B_j becomes

$$B^j = \left[1 - \frac{1}{(1 + R)^{j-1}(R + R/r_1 + 1)} \right] \left[\frac{1}{(1 + r_1)^A} \right] \quad (7\text{-}10)$$

A tabulation of B^j, for alternative values of r_1 and R, with $A = 20$ and $j = 10$ (note that this is the principal projection period of this study) is presented in Table 7-1.

Table 7-1. Index of the Short-range Bias of the Gross Capital-output Coefficient B^{10}, for $A = 20$, times 100 (i.e., per cent)

$R =$	-0.02	0	0.02	0.04	0.06	0.08
$r_1 = 0.02$	x	0	38	50	56	59
0.04	-63	0	20	29	34	37
0.06	-25	0	12	18	22	24
0.08	-13	0	8	12	15	17

For example, consulting the percentage in the third row and the third column of Table 7-1, we find that using a historical coefficient to evaluate gross investment 10 years hence, with 2 per cent acceleration over the base period (that is, from 6 to about 8 per cent growth rate), will overestimate the magnitude sought by 12 per cent; in other words, the true investment level will be 88 per cent of the level actually estimated.

As could be expected from the pattern revealed by Figure 9, the biases involved are the more serious, the lower the initial rate of growth r_1 and the greater the acceleration (deceleration) R. Indeed, using for prediction gross capital coefficients derived for a period of low rate of growth, in situations where a significant acceleration (or deceleration) is expected, is nothing better than futile.

A rather interesting fact—not intuitively obvious—is revealed by the tabulation of the long-range index of bias B^{∞}, corresponding to the same parameters as those used in constructing Table 7-1 except, of course, for the parameter j, which now equals infinity. (See Table 7-2.)

Except for the lowest initial rate ($r_1 = 0.02$) with small accelerations or decelerations, the short- and long-range biases can be taken for the practical purpose of the present study as identical. Of course, the region of approximate equality will be affected somewhat by the level of A and also by the length of the projection period j. However, these changes

Table 7-2. Index of the Long-range Bias of the Gross Capital-output Coefficient B^{∞}, for $A = 20$, times 100 (i.e., per cent)

$R =$	-0.02	0	0.02	0.04	0.06	0.08
$r_1 = 0.02$	x	0	27	50	56	59
0.04	-43	0	19	29	34	37
0.06	-25	0	11	18	22	24
0.08	-13	0	8	12	15	17

of the relationship between B^j and B^∞ always remain relatively small compared with the component of the bias common to both indices.

The computational advantage of B^∞ over B^j is not really very significant, and consequently it ought to be preferable always to compute the index actually desired without using the approximation just pointed out. The real importance of what has been said resides in its bearing on the third type of bias discussed earlier. If for a predominant class of situations the two biases B^j (j finite, shorter than A) and B^∞ remain close to each other, then, as pointed out previously, the possible bias in deriving K_1^∞ from observed data also should not be very large. Note, for example, that if an acceleration or a deceleration occurred over the preceding period, then what actually is being estimated in the sample period is some coefficient of the type K^j (rather than the K^∞ sought); but we have at least approximate evidence that K^j and K^∞ will not be too far apart, unless the rate of growth in the preceding period (i.e., period preceding the sample period) was very low.[3]

Before concluding this chapter it is necessary to return briefly to one important subject: the effect of other factors, primarily labor, on the marginal productivity of capital and hence on the capital coefficient which we use for prediction of future investment and import requirements. In fact, explaining increments in output only through proportional additions to capital stock is a procedure that neglects the existence of other productive factors. It also neglects the possibility that additional product could be the result of improvements in technology.

First, it can be argued that labor—especially if conceived of as a single homogeneous factor—is not really a scarce factor in most developing countries. Second, there is some empirical evidence that net capital coefficients (such as those discussed in this chapter) do not change over

---

[3] In this respect, as well as in the context of the previous discussion of short- and long-range biases, the following formula giving the short-range (true) capital coefficient as a fraction of the long-range (true) capital coefficient can be used for $j < A$:

$$\frac{K^j}{K^\infty} = \left[1 - \frac{1}{(1 + r_1 - R + r_1R)^A}\right]$$
$$\left\{\frac{r_1}{r_1 + R + r_1R}\left[\frac{1}{(1 + r_1)^A - 1}\right]\left[\frac{1}{(1 + R)^{j-1}}\right] + 1\right\}$$

where r_1 now can be interpreted either as the rate of growth in the sample period (R being the acceleration in the projection period) or as the rate of growth preceding the sample period (R being the acceleration in the sample period), and where j represents either the projection date or an average length of the sample period. For example, with both R and r_1 equal to 0.08, j equal to 10, and A equal to 20, the formula gives (approximately) 0.99. In other words the "17" in the lower right-hand corner of Table 7-1 is about 1 per cent smaller than the corresponding "17" in Table 7-2. Note also that with no acceleration, that is, with $R = 0$, the ratio K^j/K^∞ becomes equal to one, as could be expected.

time in a way that would suggest a significant impact of other scarce factors.   And finally, the most potent argument in defense of the procedure employed and suggested in this study is that the statistical information we have for most, if not all, developing countries does not permit more refined procedures of estimation.

Nonetheless, it is possible to pursue the questions just raised a good deal further on the theoretical plane and to learn at least something from an abstract analysis.   The author attempts a first step in that direction in Appendix C.   Although in its entirety the analysis presented in the appendix stands on its own and is not directly related to the mainstream of this study, at least two of its general conclusions should be stated here: (1) For any values of the underlying parameters that are at least approximately realistic, the effects of the alternative theory (i.e., formation of national product involving capital, as well as labor inputs and technological change) on the size of the predicted capital-output coefficient can be extremely significant; (2) especially if an acceleration in the rate of growth for the projection period is postulated (as in our key estimates B and D), the alternative theory leads to estimates of necessary future investment considerably higher than those obtained through the procedure offered in this study.

Chapter **8** SAVINGS AND THE TERMS OF TRADE: ALTERNATIVE HYPOTHESES

As part of our estimation procedure we have used the terms of trade of Colombia as an explanatory factor of the propensity to save (see section 3-2). It will be recalled that the relation between the average propensity to save and the terms of trade was found definitely statistically significant, and, as such, it was used in estimating future savings rates in Colombia. With the exception of a brief statement of a hypothesis that such a relation could depend on the policy of (internal) export price stabilization, we have not made any attempt to justify or explain the relationship on a priori grounds. And yet, such an explanation, actually a comprehensive analysis of the relationships among all the variables involved, is called for if we are to trust the particular statistical relationship and make intelligent use of it for prediction.

At least three standard hypotheses (theories) of savings behavior come to mind in respect to our terms-of-trade–savings relation. Unfortunately, none of the three is very satisfactory. The first is the Keynesian savings function; the second is a savings function based on the so-called permanent-income hypothesis; and the third puts most of the burden of the explanation on the way in which savings and other major national income aggregates actually are recorded in the less developed countries.

Recalling the explicit form of the relation discussed [see relation (3-10)], we first observe that the average and marginal savings rates with terms of trade constant are the same. However, with a change in the terms of trade, a change that makes income move in the same direction, the average savings rate is altered considerably. If the only effect of the terms of trade on savings were that which operates through income, it could be expected that the dependent variable would at least approximately equal a constant, no significant explanatory value being attributable to the terms of trade.

At first sight the permanent-income hypothesis seems to be more satisfactory: average and marginal savings rates (by implication, consumption rates) are approximately identical with unchanging terms of trade, and the terms of trade can be taken as transitory random shocks which, in expectation of a given level of permanent income, leave consumption essentially unchanged and thus heavily influence the average savings rates. The difficulty with this explanation is that with a decline in the terms of trade over a span of 10 years or so, one could expect a certain adjustment in the permanent-income expectation, and thus an upward readjustment in the average propensity to save after many years of unfavorable terms of trade. No such thing can be detected in the sample used. Of course, it must be admitted that our data and definitions are so crude that the interpretations cannot be attributed a final validity.

As for our third hypothesis, the argument is often advanced that in most less developed countries, including Colombia, the savings aggregate, or at least some part of it, is estimated as a residual from an evaluation of investment and of the balance of payments on current account. If then the terms of trade decline considerably, the balance of payments is normally expected to deteriorate, and thus, to the extent that the country in question carries out a pre-set investment program, total savings must decline. Whereas this hypothesis describes adequately in some instances what actually happens, it does not explain the phenomenon at hand.

However, the hypothesis is not entirely without value. If more carefully explored, in the full context of a developing economy, it allows us to learn a good deal more about the process whereby fluctuations in the terms of trade are translated into fluctuations in average savings rates. To this effect, let us use the modification of a conventional trade diagram presented in Figure 10. The modification consists in the introduction of a larger number of products—or commodity groups—and in the possibility of considering situations other than those of balance of payments

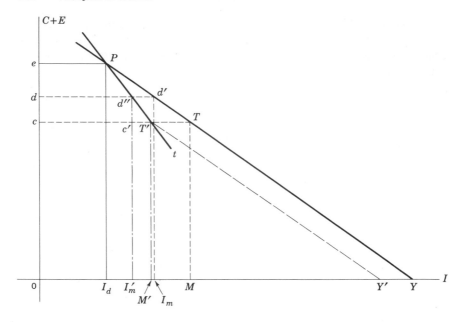

Figure 10. A diagrammatic representation of the relationship between the terms of trade and savings.

equilibrium; both alterations are introduced to describe a developing economy more truthfully than a conventional trade diagram.

Consider first the initial situation (before the terms of trade deteriorate). The economy produces three types of products (and/or services): (1) produce for consumption Oc; (2) produce for exports ce; and (3) the domestic component of total gross investment OI_d. The economy imports two types of products: (1) investment goods I_dI_m; and (2) goods that enter directly, or indirectly as intermediate products and raw materials, the internal consumption of the economy I_mM.

Now to deal with five commodity aggregates in a two-dimensional diagram, special—but not too unrealistic—assumptions must be made regarding valuation. First, it can be safely admitted that import products, whether capital goods or others, sell at given prices in terms of foreign currency. These products, with physical units defined as "one dollar's worth," are then taken as numeraire. The remaining aggregates measured along the horizontal axis, domestic outputs entering gross capital formation, also are measured in units of "one dollar's worth," at the going rate of exchange and at the going internal price of such products.

The domestic consumption products and export products, measured along the vertical axis, are expressed in physical units corresponding to an equal value in terms of the numeraire (as drawn in the diagram it will turn out that both are measured in terms of about "one dollar and twenty cents' worth"). The relative prices of both export and domestic consumer products (in terms of the numeraire) are given by the slope of the line PY. Because external trade takes place at that ratio, that line is also the trading line whose slope (measured from the vertical axis) is the net barter terms of trade of our hypothetical country. It follows from the construction that OY measures the money value (in terms of the dollar numeraire) of gross national product.

Because the value of exports (in terms of numeraire) is equal to the value of imports, both magnitudes being expressed by the segment I_dM, the balance of payments on current account is in equilibrium; and consequently savings equal investment, that is, OI_m in the diagram. Observe that total investment consists of domestic output (or, more precisely, value-added) entering capital formation OI_d and of products imported for investment I_dI_m. It will be observed from the diagram that de of the export products is allocated to the (barter) purchase of investment goods abroad.

Thus the dependent statistic considered in section 3-2, that is, the average savings rate, can be expressed in terms of magnitudes appearing in the diagram as OI_m/OY. On the other hand, the net barter terms of trade, which were our independent variable, are expressed by I_dY/I_dP.

Now, to study the relation between the two variables (of the type estimated empirically earlier in this study), let us assume that the net barter terms of trade deteriorate to the level indicated by the slope of Pt. We shall consider first the situation where the external balance remains in equilibrium following the terms-of-trade deterioration. It may be recalled that this situation is approximated by the Colombian experience in the early years of declining terms of trade—say, from 1954 to 1959.

Before we turn to the actual examination of the case at hand, some additional specifications must be made to avoid confusion at a later stage. First, it must be recalled that all commodities—whether consumed domestically, exported, or imported—are always measured in physical units defined above, units of one dollar's worth for products on the horizontal axis and units of somewhat greater worth for products reckoned along the vertical axis. These physical units of measurement do not change, whatever happens to prices as a result of a terms-of-trade alteration. Second, it will be observed that in our hypothetical example the production point P does not change between the two periods considered. If growth were to be assumed over the time span the terms of trade are declining, this could be conveniently taken care of by shrinking of the scales along the two axes, as was done in section 6-4. In this connection, observe that our two key statistics examined here are both ratios, and thus invariant with respect to proportional changes in scales along the two axes.

We eliminate any phenomenon of purely monetary inflation (which often actually takes place in developing countries) by assuming that import prices—that is, prices of the numeraire goods—remain constant in terms of foreign currency and that the rate of exchange changes in proportion with the expansion of money supply over and above the expansion called for by real growth, if any. For the purpose of our analysis it can thus be assumed that no inflationary expansion takes place and that the rate of exchange remains constant. Only relative price changes, with respect to the numeraire products, can thus be reflected in the diagram; and in fact, it is only such changes that interest us here. This, of course, does not prevent us from thinking of the two magnitudes entering the dependent variable OI_m/OY as two money magnitudes, in domestic or foreign currency, because any purely inflationary effect will cancel out in the ratio, that is, in the dependent variable.

With all these qualifications in mind, let us now postulate that the terms of trade decline, but except for the change in export prices (implied by the decline in the terms of trade) no relative price (and actually, assuming no monetary inflation, also no money price) changes. In the short, and perhaps in the intermediate, run, when resources cannot easily be shifted from one sector of the economy to another and no significant shift in demand from domestic to export products can be expected (note, for example, that a decline in the export price of coffee in Colombia is unlikely to increase domestic demand for coffee significantly), the equilibrium point indicating international exchange and national expenditure T will shift to position T'. Money income and income in terms of numeraire, on the assumption made, will shrink from OY to OY'. Observe that the ratio of the latter over the former magnitude is nothing but a Laspaires index of national expenditure, with the initial situation = 1.00.

If the proportion of imports for investment remains the same before and after the change in the terms of trade—as indicated in the diagram by the constancy of segments cd and de—investment, and on our assumption of balance of payments equilibrium also savings, will decline from OI_m to OI'_m. On the assumptions made, the two segments reflect savings and investment either in money terms or in terms of the numeraire. Our dependent variable, average savings rate, declines from OI_m/OY to OI'_m/OY'. As drawn in the diagram, this is a decline in the average savings rate of about 4 per cent *points*, corresponding to a decline in the terms of trade of about 40 per cent; our estimated relation leads approximately to such an expectation.

We can derive from this our first important conclusion.   If, as is often the case in an economy suffering from declining terms of trade, the government has to recur to foreign exchange rationing of resources which have become very scarce (that is, if the government has to determine the magnitudes of cd and de, in addition to not letting the balance of payments get out of equilibrium), by doing so, the government actually determines or, in a realistic context, at least heavily influences the savings rate of the economy.   The proportion of income saved in this situation actually has very little to do with individual savings behavior.

At this stage we have to recall the assumption of unchanged relative prices with the exception of the price of exports.   Only under exceptional conditions could the structural adjustment of demand within the economy to changing terms of trade lead to such a relative price stability.   Normally some changes in prices of domestic consumer and investment products relative to the numeraire could be expected, depending on income distribution, on buyers' preferences, and not in the least on the government policies actually adopted to cope with the situation.   However, as a more careful analysis will convince the reader (to be undertaken on his own), and as will also be indicated later in this chapter, such changes cannot very significantly affect the above conclusion—namely, that if the government regulates imports it thereby largely determines the average savings rate.

Now consider the constraints under which the government of our less developed country actually is operating.   This consideration will provide us with a bridge toward the other extreme situation where the allocation of foreign exchange between capital and other products is effected entirely through competitive forces.   In order to preserve the initial average savings rate, the government would have had to allocate just about all its export proceeds to imports of investment goods.   This would have reduced total investment from OI_m to only OM', effectively, in about the same proportion as the decline in national income from OY to OY'.   Now observe that the initial level of imports of noninvestment goods is I_mM.   Only if this entire portion of imports were imports of (nonessential) consumer goods could it entirely be eliminated without having disastrous consequences for the economy.   And observe that such an elimination is the condition for keeping the average savings rate constant.   Normally, a considerable proportion of the noninvestment goods imports in the less developed countries is found to be imports of raw material and other intermediate products.   If such imports were eliminated, excess capacities and underemployment of domestic resources manifold that of the intermediate imports foregone would result.   Observe further that even on the assumptions embodied in our diagram, noninvestment goods imports already had to be cut by almost

50 per cent.   In the absence of a sufficient leeway provided by elimination of nonessential imports, many a rational government would then prefer to reduce imports of investment goods more than in proportion to the decline in export earnings, that is, to augment rather than reduce or leave unchanged the segment *cd*.

Now, in the absence of selective allocation of foreign exchange resources by the authorities, the general outcome can hardly be very different; of course, we still preserve our assumption of a balance of payments equilibrium.   If we assume a constant rate of exchange, without much doubt the foreign currency will become scarce resulting from the deterioration in the terms of trade, and thus, to fulfill our assumption of competitive behavior, foreign exchange must be rationed competitively. The scarcity of foreign exchange will produce a higher equilibrium price of import products (that is, a higher price in terms of the numeraire for the same import products as those in the initial period), all import prices to domestic users or consumers increasing by the same amount. Under such conditions imports of a particular commodity will be curtailed more or less depending on whether the demand elasticity for such imports is high or low.   The lowest elasticities can generally be expected for intermediate products because such products often represent only a small fraction of total gross value of output of the using industry.   The elasticities of demand for consumer goods and investment goods are likely to be higher.   For the latter category, as mentioned earlier in this study, the elasticity can be quite high because changes in the initial cost of a project can have quite a significant impact on present value or internal rate-of-return computation.   This notion is even strengthened if we realize that the net demand (demand minus supply) for loanable funds (ideally, supply of securities) is not likely to be significantly curtailed because the possible slack in demand on the part of investors will generally be offset either by borrowing (dissaving) of the social groups having been hardest hit by the decline in export prices, or by tax collection, and/or by investment fund withdrawals by the government to finance subsidies to the depressed economic sectors.

Under such conditions, very much the same thing as is illustrated in the diagram can be expected: no special expansion in the share of investment goods imported; on the contrary, especially if in the initial situation not many consumer goods were imported, the normal expectation would be that the share of noninvestment goods would increase. And this in turn would reduce the average savings rate even further than is indicated in the diagram.

Now let us consider briefly the situation—resembling that of Colombia in the early 1960s—not where the balance of payments adjusts to unfavorable terms of trade, but rather where sufficient foreign resources are found to provide all or part of the foreign exchange lost by a terms-of-trade deterioration.   For example, if national expenditure (absorption) were to remain (after the decline in terms of trade) at point T and the internal structure of expenditures were also to remain the same, a real transfer—or net foreign borrowing—of $T'T$ (in terms of numeraire or dollars) would have to take place from abroad into the developing country.   In this situation, perhaps unrealistically implying that even the exporters' reduced purchasing power would have been fully restored, the decline in the average savings rate would be considerably greater than that considered thus far.   The new level of savings would now be OI_m minus $M'M$.   In another situation where foreign funds would be found only for financing of additional investment goods to restore the initial level of investment, the new savings rate would be OI_m, the same as in the former case with a balance of payments equilibrium.

The important point here is that only if additional foreign (borrowed) funds can be used exclusively for import of capital goods will the situation with balance of payments equilibrium lead to the same savings rate as that with a deficit.   If, however, availability of additional foreign exchange renders the authorities more lenient than they would have been otherwise with respect to noninvestment goods imports, then the savings rate must decline more resulting from a terms-of-trade deterioration than in the absence of foreign borrowing (or aid).

What has been said thus far pertains to the effects of the terms of trade on savings over a relatively short period, perhaps a three-year horizon. If terms of trade decline and remain at a low level for a prolonged period of time, as has been the case in Colombia and actually as it can be expected to be for some time in the future, the question arises as to whether other effects on the savings rate could be expected.   If budgetary and investment support from abroad could be obtained to the full extent of the segment $T'T$ in the diagram, it could be postulated that not much further structural adjustment would take place and that the low savings rate would be continued into the future as long as the terms of trade remained at a low level.

If a partial or a complete equilibration of the foreign accounts is to take place, on the other hand, no such a priori expectation can be formulated.   We have only the (at least approximate) empirical evidence for Colombia that no upward (nor for that matter downward) readjustment in the average savings rate took place after a prolonged period of declining terms of trade and a diminishing (or reduced) capacity to import.

The problem must be tackled under two headings: (1) If the government attempted to increase average savings significantly, with an equilibrium balance of payments (on current account), could it succeed? and (2) Under conditions of an approximate *laissez faire*, would there be natural forces present in the long run that would tend to bring up the average savings rate in spite of stagnant low terms of trade?   The first question is easier to answer; we can refer here to the analysis of Chapter 6.   If average savings have declined with deteriorating terms of trade, there is a strong presumption that the export-import gap (rather than the savings-investment gap) was, or has become in the course of the terms-of-trade deterioration, dominant.   Under such conditions the government can succeed in revising the savings rate only if it can increase exports and thus recapture foreign exchange earnings lost on account of lower terms of trade, or if it can substitute some intermediate or capital goods that previously had to be imported.   Without such possibilities, an attempt to increase savings, say, through increased tax-rates, might leave the savings rate unchanged and at the same time have disastrous effects on the economy, such as deflation, excess capacity, unemployment, and other effects.   On this account our empirical evidence of no upward readjustment tells us that to the extent the government of Colombia tried to increase the savings rate to offset the effects of terms-of-trade deterioration, it was, on balance, unsuccessful in doing so because of its inability—or much more likely impossibility—to expand exports or substitute for imports.

We may now turn briefly to the second heading.   Suppose that we are for a few years in the situation described in our diagram, after the terms of trade have declined.   Now assume further that the terms of trade remain at the low level indicated by the slope of PT' for, say, 10 years, while the economy may keep growing (this being approximately taken care of, as indicated, by a gradual alteration of the scales).   Under such conditions the rigid proportions of the diagram can no longer be accepted; rather, such transformations and transfers of resources as are called for by changed, or changing, relative values can be envisaged.

Several things are likely to happen.   We are provided with a convenient starting point for our discussion by considering domestic production of investments OI_d in the diagram.   This matter actually has some relevance even for the short run.   Because at least in some projects domestic investment output is complementary with imported capital goods, the restriction of imports of capital goods, resulting from a decline in the terms of trade, is likely to bring about a reduced demand for internal investment output and thus shorten the segment OI_d, while reducing relative prices and presumably profits in the investment goods industries. Thus even in the short run the adverse effect on investment and savings (note that we assume an equilibrium of the balance of payments throughout) can be increased beyond the pure import effect (that is, shrinkage of I_dI_m).   As time goes on, at least over the first few years, a tendency to transfer resources from investment industries into domestic consumer industries can be expected, reinforcing the detrimental effect of unfavorable terms of trade on the average savings rate.   The situation in the capital markets, it will be observed, is perfectly consistent with this happening, because demand for investment funds has slackened and, to the extent that excess supply of loanable funds has arisen in some sectors of the economy, it can be expected to be absorbed directly or indirectly by dissaving in the export sectors.

Thus a transfer of resources from traditional domestic investment industries into the domestic consumer goods industries can be expected in the longer run.   This tendency will only be reinforced by relatively higher internal prices of imports of consumer goods and intermediate goods directed toward consumption, also resulting from an increased scarcity of foreign exchange earnings.   In other words, there will be a natural tendency to develop import-substituting consumer goods industries (it could be expected that such a tendency would be the strongest for intermediate products).

The scarcity of foreign earnings, however, will also tend to provide an additional stimulus to capital goods industries whose outputs can substitute for equipment and machinery previously imported.   And thus, at least after several years of unfavorable terms of trade, the initial adverse effect on the domestic portion of total investment imputable to complementarity can be expected to be offset by capital goods import substitution.   Of course, a mere cancellation of the two can take quite a while.   And it will be observed that only by the time the two effects match each other in size, would OI_d in the diagram be restored to its original proportions.   At that stage, with unchanged terms of trade, most or all of the pure import effect on investment could still remain.

What we have just termed the pure import effect of the terms of trade on investment (reduction of $I_d I_m$ in the diagram) could be reduced by import substitution of intermediate consumer goods and possibly of finished consumer goods.   However, that is not a necessary, nor even a likely, outcome because such a substitution (reduction in de in favor of cd) may be offset or even more than offset by a transfer of productive resources from traditional export industries—on account of reduced prices and earnings—into domestic-oriented industries (that is, primarily a reduction in ce in favor of Oc).

In the even longer run than just implied for the transfer of resources from export to domestic industries, the picture becomes far grimmer whenever foreign demand for exports fails to match the growth of the economy.   Using again the method of shrinking scales, we can illustrate this case by the situation where scales are shrinking at the same rate for all segments of the axes except the segment ce, whose scale shrinks at a slower rate.   This is equivalent to shrinking scales at the *same* rate everywhere, with a gradual shortening of the segment *ce*, and a consequent movement of T' to the left along Tc. But such a movement, it will be observed, is equivalent for the purposes of the present analysis to a gradual further decline in the terms of trade, below the level indicated by the slope of PT'.

To conclude and summarize the discussion of long-run effects of lasting unfavorable terms of trade under conditions of balance of payments equilibrium and with (more or less) free economic forces at work, it can be said that on balance there are hardly any natural forces that would tend to restore the average savings rate to a higher level from the level attained in the short run. In other words, our empirical findings appear to be vindicated on grounds of the analysis here presented. As to what would be the tendency over extremely long periods, we do not want to attempt any conjectures; such conjectures would neither be very meaningful nor very useful.

Another concluding word may be in order. It appears from both our empirical analysis and our abstract theoretical discussion that the standard hypotheses (or theories) regarding formation of national savings, if at all correct, are of very little use in explaining savings rates of countries in early stages of development. There are what we may refer to as "structural factors" both on the side of aggregate supply and on the side of aggregate demand that play a significant, if not a dominant, role in determining savings rates of developing countries. This notion, it will be recalled, is also implicit in the analysis of Chapter 6.

Chapter **9** SUMMARY OF EVIDENCE FOR COLOMBIA

In Part 2 we laid out what we may call the quantitative raw material of our inquiry. In the preceding three chapters of Part 3, we subjected to a careful theoretical analysis the most important concepts and tools underlying, and economic phenomena suggested by, the "raw" statistical analysis. In part, Chapters 6 to 8 stand on their own, being applicable to and relevant for a class of problems reaching beyond the specific case of Colombia. In part, our theoretical analysis directly pertains to the Colombian case.

Although the quantitative analysis of Part 2 suggested topics treated in Part 3, results obtained in the latter part have not been integrated, thus far, with the quantitative analysis. Such an integration—or synthesis—is the main purpose of this chapter. Another purpose is to provide the study with a summary of principal findings. We are restricted here to the barest essentials, the author leaving it to the interested reader to turn to the various chapters and sections for a more detailed analysis, underlying reasoning, proofs of various points, and detailed tabulation of numerical results.

We shall concentrate on the projection year 1970, far enough in the future to be interesting for a projection and sufficiently near to keep at a reasonably low level the unavoidable factor of uncertainty.

There is a good deal of statistical and analytical evidence, corroborated by opinions of experts, that unless a very favorable coffee agreement is negotiated (or renegotiated) in the future no significant improvement in coffee prices, over and above the level of the prices of our base period 1959–1961, can be expected by 1970. If the outlook of no change in coffee prices is taken for granted, there is good reason to believe that the terms of trade of Colombia will remain almost unchanged between the base period and 1970.

With that expectation, the spectrum of alternative projections of Colombia's foreign resource requirements in 1970, as obtained in Part 2, ranges from about $120 million, corresponding to a 4.5 per cent rate of growth over the 1960s (see key estimate C-1), to about $530 million, corresponding to a rate of growth of 6.1 per cent (see key estimate D-2). Both of these estimates correspond to the import-export gap, on the assumption of a historical average rate of interest on borrowed foreign funds (to finance the deficits) of about, or somewhat above, 3 per cent per annum. It will be observed from key estimate C-1 that the tabulated value of the import-export gap actually is not dominant. However, we use it here on the grounds that the somewhat higher estimate of the savings-investment gap can be taken not as a minimum consistent requirement but rather as merely a consistent requirement (see sections 6-1 and 6-2).

This conclusion is based on two main arguments. First, as follows from our discussion in Chapter 8, the important role of the terms of trade in determining the rate of savings strongly suggests the dominance of the import-export gap in the past, and, with no significant improvement in the terms of trade in the future, it can be reasonably expected that this dominance will continue. The rationale for the latter deduction is also contained in Chapter 8. The second argument is institutional. With its heavy reliance on internal direct taxes and an overall satisfactory state of fiscal institutions, there is no doubt that Colombia could raise the national savings rate a good deal (certainly by more than the difference between the two gaps in key estimate C-1) by 1970 were it not for the (binding) import-export gap.

But the two extreme figures, $120 and $500 million, and the various other estimates within the spectrum (see the other key estimates), cannot be taken as anything else but what we have termed earlier in this chapter a "quantitative raw material of our inquiry." To obtain a better set of estimates of future foreign resource requirements of Colombia, we have to subject the original figures to a more careful scrutiny along the lines of the analysis presented in Chapters 6, 7, and 8.

We may start with the set of observations which are least likely to alter the initial results: they concern the relation between the terms of trade and the savings rate, studied in Chapter 8.   One important thing regarding that relation has been already noted.   The strong impact of the terms of trade on the savings rate suggests a dominance of the import-export gap; such an inference becomes especially likely to be correct in the situation—actually considered here—where the terms of trade in the projection year (1970) are expected to be no higher than just about the lowest terms of trade in the entire sample period (1952–1961).[1]

Another conclusion reached in Chapter 8 ought also to be brought to mind.   Over the 10-year projection period considered here, it seems to be reasonable to take the estimated relation between the terms of trade and the savings rate as a satisfactory explanation of what can be expected in the future.   In other words, the savings component of the key estimates is not likely to contain significant bias on account of that relation.

With these two observations in mind, we can conclude (1) that no revision in the key estimates is necessary on account of what we learn about the terms-of-trade–savings relation in Part 3 and (2) that it is actually correct to take the import-export gap as dominant (of course, on the assumption of basically unchanged terms of trade), and thus we can determine the foreign resource requirements of Colombia.

Our second conclusion is further supported by another important factor; this factor, however, strongly suggests that at least some of the key estimates presented in Part 2 are overestimates, that is, they contain a positive bias.   In other words, they contain a bias stemming from the use of a fixed gross capital-output coefficient in situations where acceleration or deceleration of (total or) sectoral growths is foreseen for the projection period.   This subject was treated in Chapter 7.

To the extent that acceleration is expected in most or all sectors for which a capital-output coefficient is used to estimate future investments, an overestimate of investment is to be expected.   Now it will be recalled that in our estimation procedure two investment aggregates, that for transportation equipment and that for machinery, appear both in the investment function and in the import function.   This is so because demand for such capital goods constitutes both a part of total investment demand and a part of total import demand.   If then a bias in the coefficient explaining these demands is present, it will affect the investment-savings gap and the import-export gap equally, and consequently,

---

[1] Note that if the terms of trade were expected to improve in 1970 by a substantial percentage, the likelihood that the investment-savings gap would become dominant in that year would be considerably greater, owing to the fact that the impact of improved terms of trade on the *ex ante* investment-savings gap is considerably smaller (a little over one-half, according to our results) than that on the import-export gap.

no change in the position of dominance of one gap over the other can be expected on account of such a bias.

But the capital-output coefficient is also used in the estimation procedure for investment in construction other than buildings [see relation (3-11)]. This aggregate appears only in the investment function, and not in the import function. To the extent, then, that an acceleration is expected in sectors on whose growth this type of construction depends, the correction of the bias will strengthen the dominance of the import-export gap. In fact, the aggregate investment estimate will have to be reduced whereas the projected level of imports will remain unaffected.

It thus follows that in situations involving acceleration (or at least no deceleration)—actually, only such situations are relevant for the key estimates presented here—(1) the import-export gap remains dominant, and (2) correction of biases has to be effected only for the import-export gap, that is, only for demand for investment in (a) machinery and (b) transportation equipment. We shall now attempt to evaluate the orders of magnitude of the biases involved; we shall do so only for the two extreme figures given earlier in this section, corresponding to the lowest and highest rates of growth of the Colombian economy, 4.5 and 6.1 per cent respectively.

The basic information pertaining to the two cases is as follows: The rates of growth whereon the two capital-output coefficients, for transport equipment and machinery respectively, are based (these rates are the r_i's from Chapter 8) are 3 and 6 per cent respectively. The rates of growth assumed for the projection period for the low growth estimate (rate of 4.5 per cent) in the transport and machinery-using sectors are 5.6 and 5.8 per cent respectively. This yields rates of acceleration R (as defined in Chapter 7) of 2.5 per cent and (virtually) zero per cent respectively. For the high growth estimate (rate of 6.1 per cent) the corresponding values of R are 3 and 2.5 per cent respectively. If we now take what we consider most likely replacement periods (A in Chapter 7), 20 and 15 years for transportation equipment and machinery respectively, the (10-year) indicators of short-range bias B^{10} (as defined in Chapter 7) are

$$B^{10}_{m,\text{low}} = 0\%$$
$$B^{10}_{tr,\text{low}} = 29\%$$
$$B^{10}_{m,\text{high}} = 17\%$$
$$B^{10}_{tr,\text{high}} = 32\%$$

where m and tr indicate the machinery-using and transportation sectors respectively and high and low correspond to the high (6.1 per cent) and low (4.5 per cent) overall growth rate estimates (that is, key estimates D-2 and C-1). These indices of (upward) bias suggest that our initial "raw" gap estimates of $120 and $530 million should be revised downward by about $60 and $200 million respectively.[2]

Thus, on grounds of the arguments presented in Chapter 7, it appears that a better estimate of future foreign resource requirements of Colombia in 1970 is about $60 million for an expected rate of growth of 4.5 per cent and about $330 million for a growth rate of 6.1 per cent.

With foreign funds forthcoming at a higher rate of interest equal to 5 per cent, the two figures would be approximately $70 and $370 million, and if free of any interest charges, about $40 and $270 million respectively. But it must be recalled that all the adjusted estimates presented thus far are estimates of the *net* foreign resource requirements. As is apparent from all the key estimates of Chapter 4, the gross resource requirements (gross borrowing) would be considerably greater in 1970. For example, the gross figure corresponding to the net resource requirement of $330 million (the high rate-of-growth estimate) is approximately $500 million. Also, the total level of foreign debt accumulated over the projection period would be quite significant. For example, on the assumption of a 6.1 per cent annual rate of expansion over the 1960s, with a 3 per cent rate of interest on borrowed funds, total public debt of Colombia would have to reach about $2.5 billion in 1970. In 1963, it will be recalled, it was only $715 million.

One subject remains to be briefly discussed before we conclude this chapter. In Chapter 6 we made the distinction between what we called the "consistent requirements" and "minimum consistent requirements." Thus far we have treated the dominant gap without attempting to identify it according to such a classification. Specifically, we are in a position to ascertain that the estimate of $60 million is consistent with a 4.5 per cent rate of growth of the Colombian economy—and, of course, the underlying growth structure—and that the estimate of $330 million is consistent with a 6.1 per cent annual growth rate. But do these estimates also represent minimum requirements?

The anatomy of the 1970 projections suggests that, given the structural and other conditions assumed to prevail, there is actually not much leeway for reducing the (adjusted) import-export gaps. Perhaps, with increased austerity in respect to imports of nonessential consumer goods, it would be possible to reduce the low growth estimate by as much as $50 million and the high growth estimate by somewhat more. It could thus be concluded that with a high degree of discipline Colombia is in a position to grow at a rate of 4.5 per cent without any significant inflow of foreign resources, and that under such conditions, Colombia would

---

[2] These are only approximate calculations, subject to a possible error of as much as $5 or even $10 million.

need somewhat less than $300 million in 1970 were it to grow at the (planned) rate of 6.1 per cent.

But it must be emphasized that if Colombia's terms of trade were to improve significantly in the future, the rate of growth usually termed as self-sustained would increase.   Just to give an illustration, the return of the terms of trade to the 1958 level (increase of about 20 per cent), that is, about one-fourth of the decline since 1954, would raise the self-sustained rate of growth from the 4.5 per cent just mentioned to about 4.8 per cent per annum for the 1960s.

APPENDIX A APPENDIX TO CHAPTER 4: DERIVATION OF THE KEY ESTIMATES

This appendix sets forth the data upon which the aggregate projections of investment, savings, imports, and exports in Chapter 4 are based. We show here the projections for each of the components of the four functions (summarized in section 3-7).

To simplify the use of the following tables a uniform set of footnotes is employed. No footnote indicates figures for: (a) no change in the terms of trade (from $T = .86$ in 1959–1961); (b) a rate of growth in the volume of Colombia's exports of coffee using the estimates of Balassa (2.8 per cent per annum); and (c) the observed linear growth of the capital goods industry ($V_3{}^m = 0.25t$ and $V_3{}^{tr} = .015t$, where $t =$ number of years from 1960). The following footnotes indicate only *deviations* from the above "norm." Hence, for example, footnote 3 indicates exponential rate of growth of the capital goods industries with no change in the terms of trade and Balassa's rate of growth of coffee exports.

Footnote 1 designates an improvement in the terms of trade to the 1958 level; in other words, for the savings·function, T returns to 1.00 (from .86), and, for the export function, assuming the improvement occurs entirely in coffee exports (with no change in other export or import prices), $P_c = 1.234$. Thus world terms of trade increase by 16.3 per cent, and world market price of Colombian coffee by 23.4 per cent.

Footnote 2 designates use of the IBRD estimate for the rate of growth

Table A-1. Projections of Investment

(Values in billions of 1960 pesos)

$Function$†	$I =$	I_b	$+ I_c$	$+ I_{tr}$	$+ I_m$	$+ I_v$
$Initial\ values$ (1959–1961 averages)	5.40	1.32	1.49	.58	1.32	.68[6]
(A) Projection on the basis of Committee of Nine (Alliance for Progress) sectoral rates						
(a) Assumptions		$r_V = .049$	$r_{234567} = .068$	$r_7 = .056$	$r_{23456} = .070$	$r_V = .040$
(b) Result, 1965	7.53	1.68	2.18	.89	2.12	.66
(c) Result, 1970	10.22	2.15	3.06	1.17	2.99	.85
	10.24³		3.07³		3.00³	
(d) Result, 1975	13.98	2.78	4.28	1.53	4.29	1.10
(B) Projection on the basis of past trends, 1959–1961						
(a) Assumptions		$r_V = .055$	$r_{234567} = .067$	$r_7 = .082$	$r_{23456} = .064$	$r_V = .055$
(b) Result, 1965	7.92	1.72	2.17	1.47	1.88	.68
(c) Result, 1970	10.90	2.25	3.01	2.18	2.57	.89
	10.92³		3.02³		2.58³	
(C) Projection on the basis of "minimum" observed trends						
(a) Assumptions		$r_V = .045$	$r_{234567} = .058$	$r_7 = .056$	$r_{23456} = .058$	$r_V = .045$
(b) Result, 1965	6.63	1.64	1.79	.89	1.66	.65
(c) Result, 1970	8.60	2.05	2.37	1.17	2.20	.81
(D) Projection on the basis of Colombia's Development Plan						
(a) Assumptions		$r_V = .061$	$r_{234567} = .083$	$r_7 = .062$	$r_{23456} = .087$	$r_V = .061$
(b) Result, 1965	9.21	1.77	2.88	1.01	2.85	.70
(c) Result, 1970	13.30	2.38	4.28	1.37	4.33	.94
	13.32³		4.29³		4.34³	

† The functions are presented in detail in section 3-7.
[6] This I_v is inflated due to unusually high inventory accumulation in 1959–1961. The expected value using our function derived from the 10-year average would have been .52.

of the volume of Colombia's coffee exports (2.2 per cent per annum).

Footnote 3 designates use of low exponential rates of growth of 15 and 10 per cent respectively for machinery and transportation equipment.

Footnote 4 designates use of high exponential rates of growth of 22 and 12 per cent (the observed, implied 1956–1961 rates) respectively for machinery and transport equipment, with a compensating reduction in the growth of sector V_4 so as to keep V_{34} growing at the rate assumed by the National Development Plan.

Footnote 5 designates growth of the capital goods industries, according to Chenery–United Nations functions, incorporating the effects of growth in income per capita and in population:

$$\Delta V_3/V_3 = 1.98\Delta Y/Y + 1.31\Delta P/P = .42$$

Table A-2. Projections of Savings

(Values in billions of 1960 pesos)

Function†	$S =$	S_d	$+ S_{gh}*$	$+ P_e$	$+ T_{yp}$	$- G$
Initial values (1959–1961 averages)	4.89	2.67	2.06	1.23	.89	1.96
(A) Projection on the basis of Committee of Nine (Alliance for Progress) sectoral rates						
(a) Assumptions		$\Delta I = at^6$	$r_V = .049^7$	$r_{234} = .064$	$r_V = .049$	$r_V = .049$
(b) Result, 1965	6.01	3.00	2.60	1.73	1.17	2.49
	6.28[1]		2.87[1]			
(c) Result, 1970	8.10	4.05	3.35	2.37	1.54	3.21
	8.61[1]		3.86[1]			
(d) Result, 1975	10.94	5.38	4.31	3.23	2.16	4.14
	11.22[8]		4.59[8]			
(B) Projection on the basis of past trends, 1959–1961						
(a) Assumptions		$\Delta I = at^9$	$r_V = .055$	$r_{234} = .062$	$r_V = .055$	$r_V = .055$
(b) Result, 1965	6.10	3.06	2.67	1.72	1.21	2.56
(c) Result, 1970	8.38	4.27	3.49	2.33	1.64	3.35
	8.40[3]		3.50[3]		2.35[3]	3.36[3]
(C) Projection on the basis of "minimum" observed trends						
(a) Assumptions		$\Delta I = at^{10}$	$r_V = .045$	$r_{234} = .056$	$r_V = .045$	$r_V = .045$
(b) Result, 1965	6.06	3.14	2.55	1.67	1.15	2.45
	6.46[1]		2.95[1]			
(c) Result, 1970	7.62	3.83	3.18	2.19	1.48	3.06
	8.12[1]		3.68[1]			
(D) Projection on the basis of Colombia's Development Plan						
(a) Assumptions		$\Delta I = at^{11}$	$r_V = .061$	$r_{234} = .087$	$r_V = .061$	$r_V = .061$
(b) Result, 1965	6.86	3.62	2.74	1.88	1.25	2.63
	7.29[1]		3.17[1]			
(c) Result, 1970	10.10	5.42	3.69	2.78	1.75	3.54
	10.12[3]		3.70[3]	2.80[3]		3.55[3]
	10.69[3,1]		4.27[3,1]			

† All the functions are presented in detail in section 3-7.
[6] Assuming a linear rate of growth of gross domestic fixed investment yields $a = .43$ between 1960 and 1965, $a = .50$ between 1965 and 1970, and $a = .70$ between 1970 and 1975.
[7] This rate becomes .050 and .051 respectively in 1970 and 1975 with the given sectoral assumptions. Similar minor changes occur in some of the other rates but are not noted.
[8] Assumes no further change in the terms of trade from 1970.
[9] $a = .50$ between 1960 and 1965, $= .55$ between 1965 and 1970.
[10] $a = .25$ between 1960 and 1965, $= .39$ between 1965 and 1970.
[11] $a = .76$ between 1960 and 1965, $= .82$ between 1965 and 1970.

in 1965, .89 in 1970, and 1.44 in 1975, where Y is income per capita and P is population.   (See UN, *A Study of Industrial Growth*, 1963, p. 13.)

These footnotes will not be described again at the end of each table. All other comments, peculiar to each table, will be noted as usual at the end of the relevant table.

Table A-3. Projections of Imports

(Values in billions of 1960 pesos)

Function†	$M =$	M_r	$+ M_f$	$+ M_{bm}$	$+ M_m$	$+ M_{tr}$	$+ M_o$	$+ M_{s1}$	$+ M_{s2}$
Initial values (1959–1961 averages)	4.36	.26	.10	.29	1.01	.39	1.29	.80	.22
(A) Projection on the basis of Committee of Nine (Alliance for Progress) sectoral rates									
(a) Assumptions		$r_{34} = .064$	$r_{3467} = .065$	$r_{345} = .068$	$r_{22456} = .070$	$r_7 = .056$	$r_V = .049$		$r_W = .051$
(b) Result, 1965	5.68	.35	.14	.40	1.49	.52	1.64	.85	.28
	5.61[3]				1.41[3]	.53[3]			
	5.83[5]				1.60[5]	.56[5]			
(c) Result, 1970	7.30	.48	.19	.56	2.08	.65	2.08	.90	.36
	6.74[3]				1.58[3]	.59[3]			
	7.60[5]				2.29[5]	.74[5]			
(d) Result, 1975	9.88	.68	.25	.79	3.10	.86	2.72	1.02	.46
(B) Projection on the basis of past trends, 1959–1961									
(a) Assumptions		$r_{34} = .067$	$r_{3467} = .073$	$r_{345} = .065$	$r_{23456} = .064$	$r_7 = .082$	$r_V = .055$		$r_W = .051$
(b) Result, 1965	6.11	.37	.14	.42	1.25	1.10	1.69	.86	.28
	6.04[3]				1.17[3]	1.11[3]			
(c) Result, 1970	8.08	.51	.20	.57	1.65	1.66	2.21	.92	.36
	7.54[3]	.52[3]		.58[3]	1.15[3]	1.60[3]			
(C) Projection on the basis of "minimum" observed rates									
(a) Assumptions		$r_{34} = .059$	$r_{3467} = .060$	$r_{345} = .059$	$r_{23456} = .059$	$r_7 = .058$	$r_V = .045$		$r_W = .051$
(b) Result, 1965	5.30	.36	.13	.40	1.03	.64	1.61	.85	.28
(c) Result, 1970	6.61	.48	.18	.54	1.28	.85	2.01	.91	.36

(D) Projection on the Basis of
Colombia's Development Plan

	$r_{34} = .083$	$r_{3467} = .081$	$r_{345} = .087$	$r_{23456} = .087$	$r_7 = .062$	$r_{Y\cdot} = .061$	$r_{Y\cdot} = .061$	$r_{Y\cdot} = .061$	$r_{W} = .051$
(a) Assumptions									
(b) Result, 1965	6.73	.40	.14	.46	2.22	.64	1.73	.86	.28
	6.66[3]				2.14[3]	.65[3]			
	6.37[4]				1.89[4]	.61[4]			
(c) Result, 1970	9.39	.60	.21	.69	3.42	.85	2.33	.93	.36
	8.83[3]				2.92[3]	.79[3]			
	7.54[4]				1.75[4]	.67[4]			

† The functions are presented in detail in section 3-7.

Table A-4. Projections of Exports

(Values in billions of 1960 pesos)

Function †	$E =$	E_c	$+E_p$	$+E_o$	$+E_s$
Initial values (1959–1961 *averages*)	3.97	2.24	.54	.57	.62

(A) Projection on the basis of Committee
of Nine (Alliance for Progress)
sectoral rates[8]

    (*a*) Assumptions

$$\Delta X_p = 20.6,[6]$$
$$\Delta V/V = .270[7]$$
$$(1965);$$
$$\Delta X_p = 36.8,[6]$$
$$\Delta V/V = .613$$
$$(1970)$$

(*b*) Result, 1965	4.87	2.57	.62	.81	.87
	5.16[1]	2.86[1]			
	4.80[2]	2.50[2]			
(*c*) Result, 1970	5.89	2.95	.56	1.16	1.22
	6.59[1]	3.65[1]			
	5.72[2]	2.78[2]			
(*d*) Result, 1975	7.32	3.39	.56[9]	1.66	1.71

(B) Projection on the basis of past trends,
1959–1961

    (*a*) Assumptions

$$\Delta V/V = .305$$
$$(1965);$$
$$\Delta V/V = .707$$
$$(1970)$$

(*b*) Result, 1965	4.84	2.57	.59	.81	.87
(*c*) Result, 1970	5.81	2.95	.48	1.16	1.22

(C) Projection on the basis of "minimum" observed rates

    (*a*) Assumptions

$$\Delta V/V = .247$$
$$(1965);$$
$$\Delta V/V = .556$$
$$(1970)$$

(*b*) Result, 1965	4.89	2.57	.64	.81	.87
	5.18[1]	2.86[1]			
(*c*) Result, 1970	5.95	2.95	.62	1.16	1.22
	6.65[1]	3.65[1]			

(D) Projection on the basis of Colombia's
Development Plan

    (*a*) Assumptions

$$\Delta V/V = .341$$
$$(1965);$$
$$\Delta V/V = .803$$
$$(1970)$$

Table A-4. Projections of Exports (Continued)

Function†	$E =$	E_c	$+E_p$	$+E_o$	$+E_s$
Initial values (1959–1961 *averages*)	3.97	2.24	.54	.57	.62
(b) Result, 1965	4.80	2.57	.55	.81	.87
	5.09[1]	2.86[1]			
(c) Result, 1970	5.72	2.95	.39	1.16	1.22
	6.42[1]	3.65[1]			

† The functions are presented in detail in section 3-7.

[6] Assumes predicted expansion of capacity by 1965 (9.1 billion barrels) and 1970 (20.0 billion barrels) as new fields are expected to be opened.   Also, 20 per cent of present underutilization of capacity is assumed to be overcome, one-half by 1965 and completely by 1970 (IBRD estimates).   This is assumed (but not repeated) for all projections, A, B, C, and D.

[7] Implied $\Delta V/V = .270$ for 1965, etc.

[8] $P_c = P_p = 1.00 = $ 1959–1961 average, except where specified otherwise.

[9] We have no information for projecting Colombia's petroleum production beyond 1970.   There likely will be further but slower expansion.   However, since the income elasticity will decrease, tending to counteract any favorable effects from the former, we make the somewhat arbitrary assumption that petroleum exports remain at the 1970 level.

APPENDIX B APPENDIX TO SECTION 5-1: COMPUTATION OF TRANSFORMATION ELASTICITIES FOR THE COLOMBIA ESTIMATION STRUCTURE

For reasons that were discussed in section 5-2 the sensitivity analysis was completely produced only for the key estimate A-1. In order to make it possible to compute the transformation elasticities for any of the key estimates and in order to explain the method in greater detail than was done in section 5-1, we summarize in this appendix the equations yielding numerical values of the transformation elasticities.

Using e to represent a transformation elasticity and the subscripts i, s, m, and e respectively to represent investment, savings, imports, and exports, we have for the IS gap transformation elasticity e_{is}, that is,

$$e_{is} = \frac{Ie_i - Se_s}{I - S} \tag{B-1}$$

and for the import-export gap, or B^* elasticity,

$$e_{me} = \frac{Me_m - Ee_e}{M - E} \tag{B-2}$$

where I, S, M, and E are the estimated values of the four aggregates in the projection year (that is, year for which estimates and transformation elasticities of these estimates are sought.)

Once the individual investment, savings, import, and export elasticities are known, the gap elasticities can easily be calculated. The major task then is to obtain the individual elasticities.

The transformation elasticity for, say, investment with respect to parameter a, is defined as

$$e_i = \frac{\partial I}{\partial a} \frac{a}{I} \tag{B-3}$$

—and defined similarly for the other three elasticities. Our problem then is to calculate the partial derivatives of the different functions with respect to the various parameters.

The partial derivatives for the estimation equations for Colombia are of two widely different types, one extremely simple to obtain, the other quite cumbersome. The first type includes cases where the parameter for which the elasticity is to be computed appears linearly in the estimation equations. Most structural parameters, such as average propensities to import or save and the marginal capital-output ratios, are of that type. The second type involves parameters which do not appear in a linear form. All the sectoral rates of growth are of that variety; the partial derivatives [appearing in relation (B-3)] for these parameters are listed further in this appendix.

An extremely advantageous (shortcut) method can be employed for the linear parameters, a method not calling for a separate evaluation of the partial derivatives. Suppose that, for example, the investment function is a sum of a number of terms F_1, F_2, . . . , etc. and that one term contains a capital-output coefficient K and is of the form $K \cdot d$ (where d generally will be a product of other terms whose value is known for the projection year). The investment function then can be written as

$$I = F_1 + F_2 + \cdots + K \cdot d \tag{B-4}$$

Carrying out the calculation indicated by relation (B-3) we obtain

$$e_i = \frac{K \cdot d}{I} \tag{B-5}$$

In other words, the transformation elasticity for a linear parameter is nothing but the proportion of the term in the investment function containing the linear parameter in total investment. The same holds true for the other elasticities, namely e_s, e_m, and e_e.

Consider now a situation where the linear parameter is an average or marginal propensity relating the effects of a change in an independent variable (such as sectoral or global value-added) to a combination of dependent variables (such as the property and personal income taxes in our savings relation). If it can be expected that the two components of the dependent variable (e.g., personal income taxes and property taxes) remain in constant proportion to each other, then, it will be easily seen, the transformation elasticity for an individual component of the aggregate (e.g., personal income taxes only) will be computed [similarly to relation (B-5)] as the proportion of the value of the individual component in total savings, imports, or other aggregates, in the projection year. This method is very useful in examining the effects of policy parameters on the size of the gap in situations where a given policy aggregate (such as personal income taxes) does not appear as a separate element of the estimation equations.

The partial derivatives of the estimation equations with respect to sectoral rates of growth are presented below, under separate headings for investment I, savings S, imports M, and exports E. Coefficient r_i represents the rate of growth of the ith sector ($i = 1, 2, \ldots , 8$). Coefficient d is used here to indicate partial (rather than total) differentiation. Terms in the various equations that repeat themselves for all or some of the eight sectors are indicated by dittos, it being understood that the subscript i ($= 1, 2, \ldots , 8$) changes in the different expressions.

PARTIAL DERIVATIVES OF THE INVESTMENT FUNCTION

$$\frac{dI}{dr_1} = 0.074[\bar{V}_1 t(1 + r_1)^{t-1}] + \qquad\qquad 0$$

$$\frac{dI}{dr_2} = \qquad `` \qquad] + \bar{V}_2(6.23)[(1 + r_2)^t + r_2 t(1 + r_2)^{t-1}]$$

$$\frac{dI}{dr_3} = \qquad `` \qquad ] + \bar{V}_3( \qquad `` \qquad]$$

$$\frac{dI}{dr_4} = \qquad `` \qquad ] + \bar{V}_4( \qquad `` \qquad]$$

$$\frac{dI}{dr_5} = \qquad `` \qquad ] + \bar{V}_5( \qquad `` \qquad]$$

$$\frac{dI}{dr_6} = \qquad `` \qquad ] + \bar{V}_6( \qquad `` \qquad]$$

$$\frac{dI}{dr_7} = \qquad `` \qquad] + \bar{V}_7(10.61)[(1 + r_7)^t + r_7 t(1 + r_7)^{t-1}]$$

$$\frac{dI}{dr_8} = \qquad `` \qquad] + \qquad\qquad 0$$

PARTIAL DERIVATIVES OF THE SAVINGS FUNCTION

$$\frac{dS}{dr_1} = \bar{V}_{1t}(1+r_1)^{t-1}[(0.091T+0.004)-0.079] + [1.15\bar{T}_{yt}(1+15r_1)^{t-1}]\bar{V}_1/\bar{V} + 0.2\left[0.074\bar{V}_i\sum_{j=t-5}^{j=t-1}j(1+r_i)^{j-1}\right] + \quad 1 + 0.2\left\{\bar{V}_i(6.23)\sum_{j=t-5}^{j=t-1}[(1+r_i)i + r_ij(1+r_i)^{j-1}]\right\} \quad 0$$

$$\frac{dS}{dr_2} = \bar{V}_{2t}(1+r_2)^{t-1}[(0.091T+0.004)+0.161] + [\quad|\bar{V}_2/\bar{V}+0.2[\quad\cdots\quad 1+0.2\{\quad\cdots$$

$$\frac{dS}{dr_3} = \bar{V}_{3t}(1+r_3)^{t-1}[\quad]+[\quad|\bar{V}_3/\bar{V}+0.2[\quad\cdots\quad 1+0.2\{\quad\cdots$$

$$\frac{dS}{dr_4} = \bar{V}_{4t}(1+r_4)^{t-1}[\quad]+[\quad|\bar{V}_4/\bar{V}+0.2[\quad\cdots\quad 1+0.2\{\quad\cdots$$

$$\frac{dS}{dr_5} = \bar{V}_{5t}(1+r_5)^{t-1}[(0.091T+0.004)-0.079]+[\quad|\bar{V}_5/\bar{V}+0.2[\quad\cdots\quad 1+0.2\{\quad\cdots$$

$$\frac{dS}{dr_6} = \bar{V}_{6t}(1+r_6)^{t-1}[\quad]+[\quad|\bar{V}_6/\bar{V}+0.2[\quad\cdots\quad 1+0.2\{\quad\cdots$$

$$\frac{dS}{dr_7} = \bar{V}_{7t}(1+r_7)^{t-1}[\quad]+[\quad|\bar{V}_7/\bar{V}+0.2[\quad\cdots\quad 1+0.2\left\{\bar{V}_7(10.61)\sum_{j=t-5}^{j=t-1}[(1+r_i)i + r_{ij}(1+r_i)^{j-1}]\right\}$$

$$\frac{dS}{dr_8} = \bar{V}_{8t}(1+r_8)^{t-1}[\quad]+[\quad|\bar{V}_8/\bar{V}+0.2[\quad\cdots\quad 1+\quad\cdots\quad 0$$

PARTIAL DERIVATIVES OF THE IMPORT FUNCTION

$$\frac{dM}{dr_1} = 0.052\bar{V}_i t(1 + r_i)^{t-1} + (0.25)\bar{M}_{s1} t(1 + 0.25 r_i)^{t-1}\bar{V}_i/\bar{V} + \qquad\qquad 0$$

$$\frac{dM}{dr_2} = \text{``} \qquad + 3.33\bar{V}_i[(1 + r_i)^t + r_i t(1 + r_i)^{t-1}]$$

$$\frac{dM}{dr_3} = \text{``} \qquad + \text{``} \qquad + 0.073\bar{V}_i t(1 + r_i)^{t-1} - 2.15\bar{V}_3 t(1 + r_3)^{t-1}$$

$$\frac{dM}{dr_4} = \text{``} \qquad + \text{``} \qquad + \text{``} \qquad - \qquad 0$$

$$\frac{dM}{dr_5} = \text{``} \qquad + \text{``} \qquad + 0.057\bar{V}_5 t(1 + r_5)^{t-1} - \qquad 0$$

$$\frac{dM}{dr_6} = \text{``} \qquad + \text{``} \qquad + 0.016\bar{V}_6 t(1 + r_6)^{t-1} - \qquad 0$$

$$\frac{dM}{dr_7} = \text{``} \qquad + 7.71\bar{V}_7[(1 + r_7)^t + r_7 t(1 + r_7)^{t-1}] + 0.016\bar{V}_7 t(1 + r_7)^{t-1} - \qquad 0$$

$$\frac{dM}{dr_8} = \text{``} \qquad + \qquad\qquad 0$$

PARTIAL DERIVATIVES OF THE EXPORT FUNCTION

$$\frac{dE}{dr_i} = (0.016)(2.27)(26.1)(\bar{V}_i/\bar{V})t(1 + r_i)\dagger$$

† The other term that this derivative ought to contain is numerically negligible.

APPENDIX C APPENDIX TO CHAPTER 7: THE CAPITAL-OUTPUT COEFFICIENT: VARIABLE FACTOR PROPORTIONS AND TECHNOLOGICAL CHANGE[1]

C-1 INTRODUCTION

One of the key problems in development planning is to evaluate the rate of capital formation consistent with the production targets of the plan. The approach most frequently employed in resolving this problem is to postulate a rigid relationship between annual increments in the capital stock (investment) and annual increments in output.

More recently we find in economic literature empirical attempts to explain the level of output not only through capital stock (or its increments) but also through (1) the level of input of other primary factors of production and (2) a residual imputable to technological change.[2]

[1] The author expresses his thanks to Prof. Arnold C. Harberger, who called to his attention the question treated in this appendix. The material was first prepared for a conference on Economic Development in Latin America, held at Cornell University in April, 1966, with the assistance of Mr. Trent J. Bertrand.

[2] For example, see Bibliography, nos. 11 and 12.

The principal purpose of our analysis is to study in abstract terms the relation between results obtained from the two alternative approaches. Specifically, the question we want to treat is: Supposing that the second approach (explanation of output through inputs of capital, other factors, and technical change) reflects the true state of the economic world, what kind of, and how important an, error do we commit by using the first? Or alternatively, if the first approach is correct, what is the bias involved in using the second?

In the following section we use a simple theoretical model and derive from it the algebraic expressions of the bias just explained. In section C-3 these results are used in computing some illustrative actual values of the bias for alternative "realistic" values of the underlying parameters. Finally, in the concluding section we discuss briefly the comparative merits of the two approaches with special reference to planning procedures for developing countries.

C-2   THEORETICAL ANALYSIS

Suppose that the total product of an economy or a sector thereof Y can be explained as a Cobb-Douglas function subject to autonomous technological progress at the constant rate a, that is,

$$Y = Ae^{at}K^{\phi}N^{1-\phi} \tag{C-1}$$

where A is a constant and K and N are homogeneous inputs of capital and labor respectively. The symbol ϕ, as is well known, is the competitive income share of capital in total product. To describe the planning problem outlined in the preceding section, let us make $t = 0$ correspond to the planning base period, and let us postulate a constant exponential rate of growth of the labor input n and a desired future rate of growth of total product (income) y. Also, without loss of generality the units of measuring K and N can be selected in such a way as to have for the base period both N_0 and K_0 equal to one; in that case, from relation (C-1), $Y_0 = A$. Given all these specifications, we can solve relation (C-1) for K and obtain

$$K(t) = e^{(y-a-n+n\phi)t/\phi} \tag{C-2}$$

wherefrom

$$\dot{K} = \left(\frac{dK}{dt}\right) = [(y - a - n + n\phi)e\phi]e^{(y-a-n+n\phi)t/\phi} \tag{C-3}$$

Now recalling that

$$Y(t) = Ae^{yt} \tag{C-4}$$

we have

$$\dot{Y} = Aye^{yt} \tag{C-5}$$

The definition of a marginal capital-output coefficient being

$$B = \frac{\dot{K}}{\dot{Y}} \tag{C-6}$$

we finally obtain our key result, using relations (C-3) and (C-5), namely,

$$B = A^{-1}\frac{1 - [a + n(1 - \phi)]/y}{\phi}\,e^{[(y-a-n+n\phi)/\phi-y]t} \tag{C-7}$$

We immediately see that given the production function (C-1), the capital-output coefficient B cannot be constant over time unless the exponent of e in relation (C-7) is zero, that is, unless y is equal to the natural rate of growth of income $\bar{y}$ defined as

$$\bar{y} = n + \frac{a}{1 - \phi} \tag{C-8}$$

For a prescribed y, B will be declining whenever $y < \bar{y}$ and will be increasing over time when $y > \bar{y}$.

But let us turn to our specific problem (prediction of consistent investment requirements) which actually involves two alternative constant levels of y: (1) that observed in the base period y_0 and (2) that postulated to prevail over the plan period y_1. Corresponding to y_0 we have the "empirical" coefficient B_0 linked to y_0 through relation (C-7) where $t = 0$. It is B_0 that is assumed constant in the future under our first planning alternative (see section C-1). On the other hand, future investment requirements using the second planning alternative are given by B_1, computed from relation (C-7) for a prescribed future period t and an assumed future y_1. For selected combinations of values of parameters A, y, n, ϕ, a, and t we compute in the following section illustrative values of an index of planning bias I, defined as

$$I = 1 - \frac{B_1}{B_0} \tag{C-9}$$

But before we turn to these results, we should make a few general observations. First, it will be noted that the bias I generally will be caused by two different forces. On the one hand, B will change from its observed base-period value on account of the exponent of e in relation (C-7). Only if the projected rate y_1 equals the natural rate of growth of income (and capital) will this component of the bias be absent. In all other cases B will be increasing or declining over time depending on the conditions stated following relation (C-8). On the other hand, whenever the historical rate of growth of income y_0 is different from the projected rate y_1, the constant multiplying e in relation (C-7) will change value between the base period and the projection period on account of the change in y from y_0 to y_1. For example, for what we may call realistic values of a, n, and ϕ, that is, 0.01, 0.02, and 0.25 respectively, with a change in y from 0.04 to 0.05 (that is, an increase of 25 per cent) between the base and the projection periods, the constant changes from A^{-1} 1.56 to A^{-1} 2.00, that is, by about 28 per cent.

Another thing that ought to be pointed out is that relation (C-7) provides us with a rough way of evaluating the technical-change coefficient a from observed data for the base period, all of which, except possibly for an estimate of total capital stock, are always easily obtainable; note that for $t = 0$ relation (C-7) has an easy solution for a in terms of observable data. It will be recalled in this connection that A is the total product in the base period measured in terms of the total capital stock in that period. Besides the ease of computation, the significant advantage of this formula is that it applies equally to situations of growth equilibrium (the golden-age state) and disequilibrium.

C-3   TABULATION OF NUMERICAL RESULTS

Because there are five different parameters determining the value of the investment bias I (defined in the preceding section), it would be very difficult to produce a comprehensive tabulation of numerical values of I for alternative values of these parameters. Instead, Table C-1 presents the values of $I = 1 - B_1/B_0$, where (from the preceding section)

$$\frac{B_1}{B_0} = Ce^{Dt} \tag{C-10}$$

for $t = 10$ and for alternative "realistic" values of C and D. C and D are defined as

$$C = \frac{1 - (a + n - n\phi)/y_1}{1 - (a + n - n\phi)/y_0} \tag{C-11}$$

and

$$D = (y_1 - n)\left(\frac{1}{\phi} - 1\right) - \frac{a}{\phi} \tag{C-12}$$

To use the table it is necessary first to evaluate C and D from the values of parameters a, n, ϕ, y_0, and y_1. Very approximate results for $t = 5$ and $t = 15$ (and similarly for other target-planning periods) can be obtained from numbers I_i in the ith column of the table by obtaining the corre-

Table C-1. Investment Planning Bias $I = 1 - B_1/B_0$† for 10-year Projections

$$\frac{B_1}{B_0} = C e^{D \cdot 10} \qquad C = \frac{1 - (a + n - n\phi)/y_1}{1 - (a + n - n\phi)/y_0} \qquad D = (y_1 - n)\left(\frac{1}{\phi} - 1\right) - \frac{a}{\phi}$$

Notations:
y_0 = historical growth rate of net product
y_1 = desired future growth rate of net product
a = rate of autonomous technical progress
n = rate of growth of labor force
ϕ = competitive income share of capital

C	D = −.05	−.04	−.03	−.02	−.01	0	.005	.010	.015	.020	.025	.030	.035	.040	.045	.050	.055	.060	.065	.070	.075	.080	.085	.090	.095	.100
.85	.49	.44	.37	.31	.23	.15	.11	.06	.01	−.04	−.09	−.14	−.20	−.26	−.32	−.39	−.45	−.52	−.60	−.67	−.75	−.84	−.92	−1.01	−1.11	−1.20
.90	.46	.40	.34	.27	.19	.10	.06	.01	−.04	−.10	−.15	−.21	−.27	−.33	−.40	−.47	−.54	−.61	−.69	−.77	−.85	−.94	−1.03	−1.13	−1.23	−1.33
.95	.43	.37	.30	.22	.14	.05	.00	−.05	−.10	−.16	−.22	−.28	−.34	−.41	−.47	−.55	−.62	−.70	−.79	−.87	−.96	−1.05	−1.15	−1.25	−1.36	−1.46
1.00	.40	.33	.26	.18	.10	0	−.05	−.10	−.16	−.22	−.28	−.34	−.41	−.48	−.55	−.63	−.71	−.79	−.88	−.97	−1.06	−1.16	−1.26	−1.37	−1.48	−1.59
1.05	.37	.30	.23	.14	.05	−.05	−.10	−.16	−.22	−.28	−.34	−.40	−.48	−.55	−.63	−.71	−.79	−.88	−.97	−1.07	−1.16	−1.27	−1.37	−1.49	−1.60	−1.72
1.10	.34	.27	.19	.10	.01	−.10	−.16	−.21	−.27	−.34	−.41	−.48	−.55	−.63	−.71	−.79	−.88	−.97	−1.07	−1.17	−1.27	−1.38	−1.49	−1.61	−1.73	−1.85
1.15	.31	.24	.15	.06	−.04	−.15	−.21	−.27	−.33	−.40	−.47	−.54	−.62	−.70	−.78	−.87	−.96	−1.06	−1.16	−1.27	−1.37	−1.48	−1.60	−1.73	−1.85	−1.98
1.20	.28	.20	.11	.02	−.09	−.20	−.26	−.33	−.39	−.46	−.54	−.61	−.69	−.78	−.86	−.96	−1.05	−1.15	−1.26	−1.36	−1.47	−1.59	−1.71	−1.84	−1.98	−2.11
1.25	.25	.17	.07	−.02	−.13	−.25	−.31	−.38	−.45	−.53	−.60	−.68	−.76	−.85	−.94	−1.04	−1.14	−1.24	−1.35	−1.46	−1.58	−1.70	−1.83	−1.96	−2.10	−2.24
1.30	.22	.14	.04	−.06	−.18	−.30	−.37	−.44	−.51	−.59	−.67	−.75	−.83	−.92	−1.02	−1.12	−1.22	−1.31	−1.44	−1.56	−1.68	−1.81	−1.94	−2.08	−2.22	−2.37
1.35	.19	.10	.00	−.10	−.22	−.35	−.42	−.49	−.57	−.65	−.73	−.81	−.90	−.99	−1.10	−1.20	−1.31	−1.42	−1.54	−1.66	−1.78	−1.92	−2.05	−2.20	−2.35	−2.50
1.40	.16	.07	−.03	−.14	−.27	−.40	−.47	−.55	−.62	−.71	−.79	−.88	−.97	−1.07	−1.17	−1.28	−1.39	−1.51	−1.63	−1.76	−1.88	−2.02	−2.16	−2.32	−2.47	−2.63
1.45	.13	.04	−.07	−.19	−.31	−.45	−.52	−.60	−.68	−.77	−.86	−.95	−1.04	−1.15	−1.25	−1.36	−1.48	−1.60	−1.73	−1.86	−1.99	−2.13	−2.28	−2.44	−2.59	−2.76
1.50	.10	.00	−.11	−.23	−.36	−.50	−.58	−.66	−.74	−.83	−.92	−1.01	−1.12	−1.22	−1.33	−1.45	−1.56	−1.69	−1.82	−1.96	−2.09	−2.24	−2.39	−2.56	−2.72	−2.89
1.60	.04	−.06	−.18	−.31	−.45	−.60	−.68	−.77	−.85	−.95	−1.05	−1.15	−1.26	−1.37	−1.48	−1.61	−1.73	−1.86	−2.01	−2.15	−2.30	−2.46	−2.62	−2.79	−2.97	−3.15
1.70	0.02	−.13	−.25	−.39	−.54	−.70	−.79	−.88	−.97	−1.07	−1.18	−1.28	−1.40	−1.52	−1.64	−1.77	−1.90	−2.04	−2.20	−2.35	−2.50	−2.67	−2.84	−3.03	−3.21	−3.41

† B_0 is the observed marginal capital-output coefficient in the base period, and B_1 the coefficient applicable 10 years later, assuming an aggregate Cobb-Douglas production function with autonomous technical change at rate a.

sponding $B_1/B_0 = I_i + 1$, multiplying that number by $1 - 5D_i$ and $1 + 5D_i$ respectively, and substituting such results into the formula for $I (= 1 - B_1/B_0)$.

As an illustration, partly based on approximate values of parameters drawn from the situation of Colombia around 1960, let us compute the investment bias for 1970, corresponding to an acceleration of the rate of growth of national product from $y_0 = 0.05$ to $y_1 = 0.06$. The other parameters we use are $n = 0.025$, $\phi = 0.3$, and $a = 0.005$.[3]

With these values of the parameters, $C = 1.45$ and $D = 0.061$; using our table, the index of planning bias becomes approximately $I = -1.60$. We may recall the exact meaning and interpretation of this number. Given the assumed technology [relation (C-1)], use of the (observed) base-period marginal capital-output coefficient in predicting investment needs 10 years in the future (given the change in y from 5 to 6 per cent) will involve a negative bias (measured in terms of the empirical coefficient B_0) of 160 per cent. In other words, on the assumptions made, the "true" investment needs are 160 per cent higher than those estimated through an unchanged coefficient B_0. Alternatively, if B_0 were the true coefficient, invariant over time, the use of B_1, and of the underlying theory of production, for prediction would involve a positive bias of 160 per cent.

C-4   THE TWO APPROACHES APPRAISED

The illustrative number just produced for what we may term "reasonable" values of the underlying parameters provides us with a suitable point of departure for the present discussion. The estimate indicates that if the economy of Colombia were to grow at 6 per cent per annum over the 1960s, by 1970 it should invest per unit of additional output 260 per cent of the 1960 investment. In other words, total investment in Colombia in 1970 should be based on a capital coefficient 160 per cent higher than it was in 1960. This figure is hard to accept for anyone who has performed measurements of the capital coefficient for alternative periods in a given country, and so is, in its present rudimentary form, the underlying theory of national product formation in developing countries. But this contention calls for some additional elaboration.

One important flaw in the Cobb-Douglas type of explanation of national product for a developing country is the treatment of the labor force as a scarce factor whose scarcity generates a significant rate of

[3] We can estimate this parameter from base-period data, as indicated in the preceding section, using the assumption that in the base period productive capital stock of Colombia was about $1\frac{1}{2}$ times the national product. If $K_0 = Y_0$, a would be exactly zero.

capital-labor substitution over time.   Another flaw is the use of the observed income share of capital ϕ (which, by the way, is not changing very fast over time, and hence the description of the productive process through a Cobb-Douglas function cannot be questioned on account of ϕ's instability) for reflecting the true marginal productivity of capital; note that with a higher ϕ, C [in relation (C-11)] certainly will be reduced and D [in relation (C-11)] most likely will be reduced, both effects contributing to a reduction of the bias.   Third, it seems to the author incorrect to treat the rate of technological change a as a constant.   With a higher rate of growth of income and hence of gross capital formation, technological change in a developing country should accelerate.   Again, considering relations (C-11) and (C-12), a positive correlation between y_1 and a tends to reduce (the absolute value of) I through reduced (absolute) values of both C and D.

All this leads to the conclusion that what we termed the second approach in section C-1 is not the proper way of estimating future investment requirements.   At the same time, except that we can safely say that the first approach is preferable, our analysis does not leave us with an excellent impression of the first approach.   Our principal excuse for using it is the lack of a better method.   Another advantage is that the first approach lends itself better than the second approach to the sectoral—or structural—estimation of investment needs adopted in the main part of this study.

The one concrete conclusion relevant for our study of Colombia is that for the high-growth-rate alternatives (especially key estimates D) our estimates, as adjusted in Chapter 9 using the method explained in Chapter 7, are probably quite optimistic.   Even a small degree of the type of forces identified in this appendix should increase both gap estimates (import-export and investment-savings) for the 6 per cent growth alternative; such an effect cannot even be entirely excluded when it comes to key estimates B, corresponding to an overall rate of growth of 5.5 per cent.

BIBLIOGRAPHY

1. Alliance for Progress, Committee of Nine, *Evaluation of the General Economic and Social Development Program of Colombia*, July, 1962.
2. Balassa, Bela, *Trade Prospects for Developing Countries*, Homewood, Ill.: Richard D. Irwin, Inc., 1964.
3. Chenery, Hollis B., *Foreign Assistance and Economic Development*, Washington, D.C.: Agency for International Development, August, 1964. (An earlier version of this paper was presented at the December, 1963, meeting of the American Econometric Society in Boston.)
4. Government of Colombia, Consejo Nacional de Politica Economica y Planeacion, *Plan General de Desarrollo Economico y Social*, Cali, Colombia: Banco de la Republica, 1962.
5. Government of Colombia, Departamento Administrativo de Estadistica, *Anuario General de Estadistica, 1961*, Bogota, Colombia, 1963.
6. Government of Colombia, Departamento Administrativo de Estadistica, *Boletin Mensual de Estadistica*, March, 1964.
7. International Bank for Reconstruction and Development, *Current Economic Position and Prospects of Colombia*, Washington, D.C., May 4, 1964.
8. International Bank for Reconstruction and Development, *Economic Growth and External Debt*, vols. 1–3, Washington, D.C., March–April, 1964.
9. International Monetary Fund, *Balance of Payments Yearbook*, vols. 13–15, Washington, D.C.
10. International Monetary Fund, *International Financial Statistics*, Washington, D.C., June, 1957, and June, 1964.
11. Kendrick, John W., *Productivity Trends in the United States*, Princeton, N.J.: Princeton University Press, 1961.

12. Soloro, Robert, "Technical Change and the Aggregate Production Function," *Review of Economics and Statistics*, August, 1957.
13. Taylor, Milton C., et al., *Fiscal Reform and Development Needs in Colombia*, unpublished study, December, 1963.
14. United Nations, *The Growth of World Industry, 1938–1961*, 1963.
15. United Nations, *International Trade Statistics Yearbook*, 1954, 1957, 1958, and 1961.
16. United Nations, *A Study of Industrial Growth*, New York, 1963.
17. United Nations, *Yearbook of National Accounts Statistics*, 1962 and 1963.
18. United Nations, Economic Commission for Latin America, *Analyses and Projections of Economic Development: III, The Economic Development of Colombia*, Geneva, 1957.

INDEX